College Success for Students of Color

378.198
RIO
(TEEN)

Rios, Francisco A.

College success for students of color

10/02/24

College Success for Students of Color

A Culturally Empowered, Assets-Based Approach

Francisco A. Rios, Jacquelyn L. Bridgeman,
Angela M. Jaime, Kevin C. Roxas,
and Caskey Russell

TEACHERS COLLEGE PRESS
TEACHERS COLLEGE | COLUMBIA UNIVERSITY
NEW YORK AND LONDON

Published by Teachers College Press, 1234 Amsterdam Avenue, New York, NY 10027
Copyright © 2024 by Teachers College, Columbia University

Front cover illustrations: Tree by John Woodcock / iStock by Getty Images; Sunburst by Armagadon / Shutterstock.

All rights reserved. No part of this publication may be reproduced or transmitted in any form or by any means, electronic or mechanical, including photocopy, or any information storage and retrieval system, without permission from the publisher.

Library of Congress Cataloging-in-Publication Data is available at loc.gov

ISBN 978-0-8077-8622-2 (paper)
ISBN 978-0-8077-8623-9 (hardcover)
ISBN 978-0-8077-8265-1 (ebook)

Printed on acid-free paper
Manufactured in the United States of America

For
Indigenous Students and Students of Color
by
Indigenous Faculty and Faculty of Color

Contents

Preface: Preparing for the Journey Ahead — xiii
    Why We Wrote This Book — xiii

Acknowledgments — xv

Prologue: Beginning Your Journey — 1

1. **Introduction: Taking Your Initial Steps** — 3
       The Value of a Postsecondary Degree:
   Why *You* Should Read This Book — 3
       Educational Attainment for People of Color — 4
       Getting the Most From This Book — 6
       Terminology Around Race and Ethnicity — 8
       Other Terms of Note — 12

2. **An Assets-Based Approach: Thriving in Postsecondary Education** — 14
       Introduction to an Assets-Based Approach — 15
       You Have Assets — 16
       Our Communities Have Wealth — 17
       A Note About Theory — 19
       Deficit-Oriented Versus Asset-Oriented Theories — 21
       Cultural Capital: An Assets-Based Approach — 21
       Community Cultural Wealth — 24

Using Community Cultural Wealth to Organize
This Book: An Overview of What's to Come ... 27

3. **Aspirational Capital: Pursuing Your Dreams** ... 32
   Introduction to Aspirational Capital ... 33
   Exploring Aspirational Capital ... 33
   Introduction to the Authors ... 35
   Career Choices and Choosing a Major ... 44
   Types of Colleges and Universities ... 45
   Planning for Your Future by Choosing
   the Right Institution for You ... 48
   Ready to Apply? ... 51
   Pulling the Application Together ... 54
   Financial Planning ... 55
   End of Chapter Activity: Draft and Write
   the Application Essay ... 59

4. **Cultural (and Ancestral) Capital: Being Your Authentic Self** ... 60
   Introduction to Cultural (and Ancestral) Capital ... 61
   Exploring Cultural Capital ... 62
   A Caution About Culture, Race, and Ethnicity ... 68
   A Note About Intersectionality ... 69
   Honoring Your Cultural Assets ... 70
   Ancestral Capital ... 72
   Identifying Your Cultural Assets ... 72
   Your Cultural Capital: Pitfalls and Caveats ... 73
   Understanding the Foundations of Racism ... 74
   Strengthening Your Cultural and
   Ancestral Assets ... 79
   End of Chapter Activity: Finding Your
   Cultural Assets ... 86

5. Linguistic Capital: Valuing Your Language(s) — 88
Introduction to Linguistic Capital — 89
Exploring Linguistic Capital — 91
Your Linguistic Assets — 95
Identifying Your Linguistic Assets — 96
Your Linguistic Capital: Pitfalls and Caveats — 97
Strengthening Your Linguistic Assets — 101
End of Chapter Activity: Building Your Linguistic Assets — 104

6. Familial and Social Capital: Walking the Path . . . Together — 105
Introduction to Familial and Social Capital — 107
Exploring Familial Capital — 108
Exploring Social Capital — 111
The Importance of Familial and Social Capital in Postsecondary Education Settings — 114
Your Familial and Social Capital: Pitfalls and Caveats — 117
Ideas for Strengthening and Effectively Using Familial and Social Capital — 121
End of Chapter Activity: Recognizing and Strengthening Your Familial and Social Capital — 125

7. Political and Resistance Capital: Speaking Truth to Power — 128
Introduction to Political and Resistance Capital — 129
Exploring Political Capital — 130
Exploring Resistance Capital — 132
Your Political and Resistance Capital: Pitfalls and Caveats — 134

Strategies for Strengthening Your Political
and Resistance Capital   135

End of Chapter Activity: Build Your Knowledge
to Increase Your Power   139

8. Navigational Capital: Making the Strange Familiar   141

Introduction to Navigational Capital   142

Exploring Navigational Capital   143

Starting With the Basics   144

People You Will Most Likely Interact With
at the University   146

What Does the Institution Do for ISOCs?   152

As Former ISOCs, What We Wish We Had
Known When We Started College   156

Communicating With Professors   158

Other Important Sources of Navigational Capital   164

End of Chapter Activity: Reverse Navigating
Your Dreams   166

9. Humanization Capital: Striving and Thriving   168

Introduction to Humanization Capital   169

Exploring Humanization Capital   170

Keys to Surviving: Using and Building
Humanization Capital   172

Your Humanization Capital: Pitfalls and Caveats   174

Don't Just Survive, Thrive   175

End of Chapter Activity: Create Your
Proactive Wellness Plan   178

Conclusion: Putting It All Together—Honoring Your Assets   180

Our Parting Words   181

An Open Letter to Faculty, Staff, and Advisors on Supporting Indigenous Students and Students of Color 183

Glossary of Terms 187

References 193

Index 197

About the Authors 203

Preface
Preparing for the Journey Ahead

A *preface*, among other things, explains the purpose of a book.

The main purpose of this book is to help Indigenous Students and Students of Color to successfully navigate their journey through postsecondary education in order to achieve the success they desire for their lives. An important part of the preparation for any journey is to hear from others who have already walked the path upon which you hope to embark.

Learning from the experience of others can help you make better choices for your own life and can help you avoid learning important lessons the hard way. The experience of others can also help you see pathways along the journey that may be open to you, of which you may not have been aware. Each of our journeys is our own, and each of us must make our own path. Your path may be a bit smoother and easier with help along the way.

WHY WE WROTE THIS BOOK

The authors of this book are Indigenous Faculty and Faculty of Color who come from a variety of cultures, ethnicities, backgrounds, and experiences. As with many academic projects, we began this book project with a question. That question was: What might we share, given our many years of experience as Indigenous Faculty and Faculty of Color, to help Indigenous Students and Students of Color to not only survive but thrive in postsecondary education settings? That is, we wrote this book thinking about you, your goals and ambitions, your postsecondary success.

A related question you might be asking yourself is why are we interested in your personal success as a Student of Color? While we are committed to the individual success of all learners, we also recognize that your success is a key part of the greater success of our communities, our nation, and even our democracy.

Imagine all the potential talent that is lost when Indigenous Students and Students of Color are pushed out of high school, sometimes at alarming rates. Imagine all the potential contributions that go undeveloped when people from our racial and ethnic communities try but fail in postsecondary education, leaving, perhaps, with thousands of dollars of debt and no degree to show for it.

In short, we are interested in your personal success but also in the many ways you can and will engage in strengthening our communities. Given this, we asked ourselves, how can we not be committed to your success?

As we write this, we want to provide our best advice for Indigenous Students and Students of Color who might be pursuing a variety of postsecondary options from technical schools, community colleges, or 4-year colleges or universities. That is, when writing this book, we were thinking about the unique experiences you might have as Indigenous Students and Students of Color.

While some of the advice we provide might seem basic to you, it reflects things we did not know as we set out on our academic journeys. Some of the advice we offer is not part of what is explicitly communicated to students as they enter their postsecondary education. In short, we offer our best advice and thinking to you about how to thrive in higher education.

We offer this short caveat as well: There is more about higher education than this book, or any other, can cover. There are lots of other good resources available that offer recommendations and advice about how to succeed in higher education. We encourage you to take advantage of these resources as well.

While your journey through postsecondary education will be unique to you, one thing that is not unique is the fact that no matter who you are and where you come from, you will benefit from support along the way. This book is our attempt to provide you the best advice we can offer with the hope that we can aid you in your journey.

Acknowledgments

As with almost all things that matter, we do not come to this work believing that whatever we accomplished has been done on our own.

We acknowledge those ancestors and elders who lit the path for us, sometimes providing that example or whispering in our ears their vision about all that we can become.

We acknowledge those courageous community activists who fought with blood, sweat, and tears to expand access to postsecondary education for Indigenous Students and Students of Color... access for which we were direct beneficiaries.

We acknowledge those individuals on community campuses—students, advisors, faculty, and staff—working to ensure that Indigenous Students and Students of Color have a quality experience, including valuing who they are and what they bring once they arrive on postsecondary campuses.

And we acknowledge individuals, like you who are reading this book, who aspire to postsecondary education for their own personal and familial betterment AND who aspire to be the future leaders of our communities, states, nation, and world.

Angela would like to recognize her community, elders, and mentors for pulling her up to stand on their shoulders. She wishes to thank her amazing sons, Esai and Emiliano, for their love and support. She would also like to acknowledge the unconditional love and support from her mother, Laura. It is because of her sacrifices Angela is able to be a change agent for Indigenous people.

Caskey would like to acknowledge and thank his immediate family (Kristen Klaphake, Chet Russell, Aiden Russell) and his extended families (the Russells, the Caskeys, and the Peratroviches).

Francisco would like to thank all those individuals who inspired him by the way they supported, affirmed, and counseled Indigenous Students and Students of Color across the several postsecondary institutions where he worked. He thanks those who continue to walk with him in life: Deb, Zekial, Natalia, Thomas (Max), and Nikki.

Jacquelyn would like to thank her family for always being so loving and supportive and for making each day of her life worth living. In particular, she would like to thank her mother, Frances Price, who first taught her how to be an empowered, strong, woman of color.

Kevin has profound appreciation for his parents, Herminia G. Roxas and Oscar T. Roxas, for the deep sacrifices they made to immigrate to the United States, raise their children, and help them have access to schools and eventually higher education. He also is so very thankful for his partner, Barbara, and children, Kieran and Zaniah, for providing support and inspiration for the work he does with students and educational professionals as a professor and college dean, including this book.

Finally, we thank the professionals at Teachers College Press who have supported our efforts to bring this book to fruition. In particular, we appreciate the support we received from Brian Ellerbeck, editorial director, who guided us throughout: from idea to production of this text. Nancy Powers and the marketing team have done much to assure this book gets into as many hands as possible. Finally, we thank creative director Dave Strauss (cover design); production editor John Bylander; and digital marketing manager Emily Freyer.

Prologue
Beginning Your Journey

A *prologue* provides background (context) for a literary work.

The story about postsecondary education is ongoing. You are entering the story about Indigenous Students and Students of Color in postsecondary education at a particular social, cultural, and political moment. We all did.

Consider two different time periods.

First, the political moment of the 1960s–1980s was when many current, especially more senior, Indigenous Faculty and Faculty of Color members were attending postsecondary education. A war in Vietnam was raging. Communities of Color led the Civil Rights Movement, fighting for inclusion, access, and equal rights. In 1963, Governor George Wallace of Alabama stood in front of the doors of the University of Alabama to prevent Black students from entering. Riots occurred in cities around the nation as the frustrations of the oppressed boiled over due to lack of attention to their concerns. Martin Luther King described these riots as "the language of the unheard" (King, 1968, para. 6).

For those aspiring to earn a higher education degree in that era, student activism to end the war in Vietnam, to extend basic civil rights to all, and to open and expand admissions to postsecondary institutions for Indigenous Students and Students of Color characterized their experience.

Secondly, consider the political moment of now. The current social, cultural, and political moment is characterized by (among other things) the wide-ranging post-COVID changes, gun violence on K–12 and college campuses, student activism in support of the Black Lives Matter movement, concerns about climate change, and debates about free speech. As we write this book, the world is dealing with the Russian invasion of Ukraine, a war raging in the Middle East, and other global instances of occupation and resistance.

This moment also includes the dismantling of affirmative action by the U.S. Supreme Court, which ruled against efforts by universities to expand the diversity of their student bodies. This decision was made in the face of compelling evidence regarding persistent inequalities in postsecondary education and the significant benefits that a diverse student body provides for all students.

All of this is to say that the story of postsecondary education often has not been, and sometimes even today seems not to be, encouraging for Indigenous Students and Students of Color and their success.

Your journey into postsecondary education begins within this historical legacy and within this contemporary political moment. This is the starting point of YOUR story.

We want you to be aware of this political moment, but not to be deterred by this moment. In fact, because of this political moment we need you, more than ever, to attend and succeed (indeed thrive) in the postsecondary institution of your choosing. We need you to understand this legacy (history), to ensure it is not our trajectory (future). We need your voice, we need your leadership, and we need your vision of a world as it might be.

As you enter postsecondary schooling at this juncture of the higher education story, we are glad you have found your way to this book. We hope this book is but one of many resources that will help you reach your personal and academic goals and aspirations. Your success is our goal. Our aspiration is that you thrive at every stage of your postsecondary journey.

We stand with you as you pursue your hopes and dreams for yourself, your community, and our nation. Let's go!

ONE

Introduction
Taking Your Initial Steps

An important question you might be asking yourself is, Why pursue a postsecondary education in the first place? Accordingly, we begin this chapter by inviting you to consider the value of a postsecondary degree to you personally and for Indigenous People and People of Color more generally. We then share our suggestions about how to get the most out of this book. We end this chapter by introducing you to some key words we will use throughout the book.

THE VALUE OF A POSTSECONDARY DEGREE: WHY *YOU* SHOULD READ THIS BOOK

In the Preface, we described why we wrote this book. An equally important question you might be asking yourself is why should I read this book?

More specifically, you might ask, why embark on the pathway to a postsecondary degree at all? Consider the following as described by Khan (2021).

On a personal level, we know a postsecondary degree brings lots of benefits:

- In terms of work opportunities, students with a postsecondary degree have expanded job prospects, especially for the many jobs that require an advanced degree, and higher employment rates compared to those without a postsecondary degree.
- In terms of personal growth and development, students with a postsecondary degree develop their critical thinking abilities,

sharpen their communication skills, expand their social networks, and gain time and personal management competence.
- In terms of quality of life, students with a postsecondary degree will earn more (even after paying back student loans) over the course of their lifetime; a higher income is associated with leading a healthier life and having greater access to healthcare when needed.

We know you would agree that these advantages of a postsecondary education certainly are significant.

On a community level, Indigenous Students and Students of Color with postsecondary degrees are in a unique position to affirm and value the diversity of our nation. Postsecondary education can help you see your social and cultural group as a promise, not a problem, and oftentimes can help you understand more deeply the unique challenges that people from your shared social and cultural group experience. As a result, you can propose more effective ways to respond to such challenges.

On a national level, consider how important your success is to a healthy United States committed, at least in words and ideals, to democracy. It has been, and continues to be, true that our democracy is fragile. Witness historical and contemporary efforts aimed at curtailing the right to vote for many people. Witness historical and contemporary efforts to draw political maps so that communities of color have less chance to elect more Indigenous Candidates and Candidates of Color to office. Indeed, witness the attempt on January 6, 2021, to overthrow Congressional action to certify a new president.

A multiracial, multicultural, and educated population is critical to the success and vibrancy of Communities of Color and essential to a thriving democracy.

EDUCATIONAL ATTAINMENT FOR PEOPLE OF COLOR

Having identified just some of the ways your success is important to you, your community, and the nation, we deplore the fact that so few from our Communities of Color have been successful in postsecondary education.

Look at Figure 1.1 from data collected by the U.S. Census Bureau as of 2021. Consider 100 students from these various racial/ethnic groups who attend public or private elementary or secondary school, at some point, in the United States. By age 25, how many have not graduated with a high school diploma or General Educational Development (GED) credential? How many have only a high school diploma? How many have gone to college but not completed a degree? How many, of that 100, have received a technical or community college degree or diploma? How many have completed a bachelor's degree? How many, of the 100, have received a master's or professional degree? And how many have received a doctorate degree?

As you look at this table, what stands out to you? Consider the overall attainment rate for all groups. Consider what you learn by looking at these numbers for each racial/ethnic group. Consider comparing one group to another (White not Hispanic, for example, with Hispanic). What do you learn by looking at the numbers?

Figure 1.1. Educational Attainment of the Population 18 Years and Over, by Age, Sex, Race, and Hispanic Origin: 2020

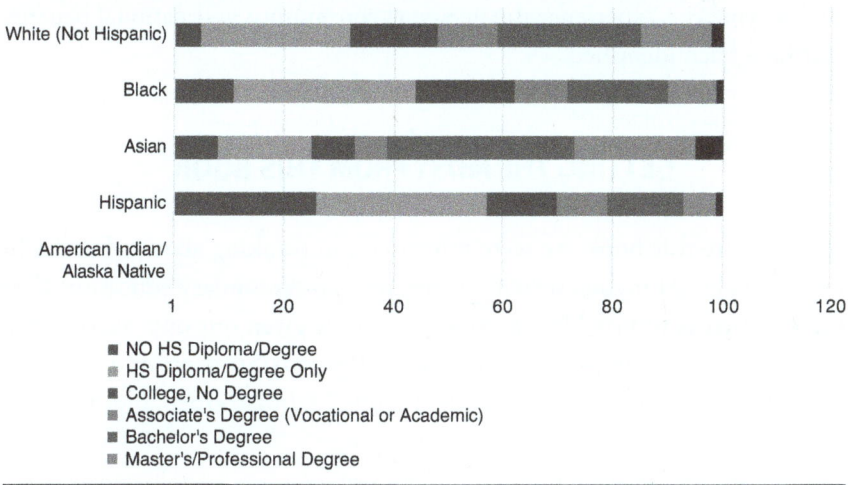

Source: United States Census Bureau (April 2021). *Educational Attainment in the United States: 2020.* https://www.census.gov/data/tables/2020/demo/educational-attainment/cps-detailed-tables.html. Author-produced figure.

At another level, what questions would you ask if you are thinking critically about these numbers? Who is represented by the term Hispanic?[1] Where would Afro-Latinx people's numbers be counted? Which groups make up the Asian category? Do members of certain Asian American communities do well in school while those from other Asian American communities struggle in academic settings? (The answer is yes.) Why are Native American and Alaska Natives not even in this data source? How did they choose to make a whole racial group's data invisible and what does that mean? And what other groups are not even represented (Middle Eastern students or immigrant students, for example)?

We encourage you to think about these questions and their implications for you as Indigenous Students and Students of Color.

However you answer the questions we have posed, consider two key ideas. First, we need to address the racial/ethnic educational attainment gaps evidenced in this data. In many ways, these are really "opportunity" gaps. Your success helps. Second, we need to develop the thinking skills that allow us to critically address the educational attainment gap. This is true for all learners. It is especially true for Indigenous Students and Students of Color, who are often on the front lines when it comes to issues of inclusion, diversity, equity, and justice. All of us must join in pursuing these aims so that all, including you, can experience the personal, community, and national benefits that have been identified.

GETTING THE MOST FROM THIS BOOK

As we wrote this book, we were purposeful in thinking about what might be most helpful for you on your journey into postsecondary education. One piece of that is to provide our collective advice given our own successes in postsecondary settings both as former Indigenous Students and Students of Color and now as Indigenous Faculty/Admistrators and Faculty/Administrators of Color.

---

[1] We use the term "Hispanic" here because that is how the data is collected. When not quoting other sources, we will use Latine throughout. We describe more about terms we use throughout this book later in this chapter.

Given our experiences, we provide our collective advice in hopes that you will find it helpful. We intend this advice to be a roadmap and source of motivation for those of you who are thinking about or are already in postsecondary institutions.

You will notice as you go through this book, that we have *italicized* some words and made others **bold**. These are words that we think are important to know. The italicized words are defined within the paragraph right after the word appears. Words that appear in bold can be found at the end of the book in the Glossary of Terms.

Also, there are several interactive features you will find in this book. We offer these to provide specific advice, to prompt thinking and discussion, and to extend your learning as you come to the end of the chapter.

- **Opening Chapter Vignettes:** To help you envision yourself in this book, we begin each chapter with a short vignette, or story, in which we imagine a group of Indigenous Students and Students of Color from diverse backgrounds, who have been friends since high school, meeting up to discuss their experiences as they consider and then pursue a variety of postsecondary institutions. We use these vignettes to illuminate many of the questions and challenges you might be facing. The vignettes are followed in the chapter by things we have learned, ideas we've gleaned, and advice we offer about navigating these questions/challenges so that you can thrive in whatever postsecondary institution you choose.
- **Think Alone/Think Together.** Throughout the book you will see prompts to "Think Alone/Think Together." These are questions that we, as Indigenous Faculty and Faculty of Color, have often thought about, sometimes alone and sometimes with others. Indeed, much of what you will be asked to do in postsecondary education is first think alone about a topic or issue and then think together either in class or with a group of your peers. Often, you will find when you think together, you are not alone in your thinking. We hope you will use these as jumping-off discussion points to engage with others reading this book, or with others you might encounter along your journey.
- **PRO TIP.** We provide a variety of "Pro Tips"—shortened from Professional Tips—throughout this book. They offer some of our

best, most direct advice that we especially want to call to your attention.
- **End of Chapter Activities.** At the end of each chapter, we offer activities you can do either alone or with a group of friends and colleagues. We intend these activities to spur critical and creative thinking skills—and extend your learning along the way—to help you understand and thrive in higher education. We hope you will use these to build on, in very practical ways, the concepts we discuss in the book.

Importantly, we invite you to use all these interactive features not only as suggestions for your individual consideration but also as jumping-off points to

- Talk with recruitment and retention specialists on your campus, especially those with a specific diversity focus, about some of the ideas presented in this book;
- Talk with Indigenous Students and Students of Color who are in their final years in postsecondary education to get their advice, wisdom, and support;
- Talk with other Indigenous Students and Students of Color who, like you, are beginning their journey in postsecondary education. These might be students with whom you are currently taking classes. Consider in particular using the "think alone" and "think together" prompts we provide regarding what will help you to thrive in postsecondary education;
- Follow up on end-of-chapter activities; and
- Share what you are learning that is contributing to your success with those around you, perhaps returning to your high school or visiting a local high school near your postsecondary campus.

TERMINOLOGY AROUND RACE AND ETHNICITY

The language we use is important. It reveals much about who we are, what we value, and how we see the world. But terminology, especially about race/

ethnicity, can be particularly tricky. The terms we use are, after all, central to our identities and that of others.

It can be tricky given that our collective efforts aimed at advancing justice are dynamic: emerging, growing, and living. Thus, our terminology is emerging, growing, and living. Given this growth, our terminology changes meaning over time. For example, consider the many ways people have sought to label Black people in the United States: Negro, African American, and Black. Consider even the recent use of the term Latinx. Advanced by younger Latina and Latino activists, the idea is to make the term Latino gender neutral. While some prefer to use Latinx, others advocate against it, preferring to use the more traditional (and probably more largely understood) terms Latino or Latina. Still others have offered the more grammatically appropriate and gender-neutral term "Latine" (the term we'll use primarily). For some, even this is still unsatisfactory.

Likewise, different terms are used in different places. Many Latine people prefer to use their specific ethnic/racial affiliation in their home community (Puerto Rican, Mexican American, or Chicano, for example) but use the more general term Latino or Latina when a variety of racial/ethnic identities with Latin American and Caribbean roots are in the same place.

Part of the challenge of using racial and ethnic labels is that they often encompass an entire group of people who may have many cultural differences, as well as differences in terms of, for example, political orientation, sexual orientation, or religious affiliation. Being lumped into an entire group by a single term can often feel like it diminishes one's specific and unique personal and racial, ethnic, and **social-cultural** (or sociocultural) identities.

We are aware of these limitations on the terms we use in society and that we use in this book. Nonetheless, we use certain terms to try to capture the many common experiences (prejudice, discrimination, colonization, resistance to oppression, etc.) people from underrepresented sociocultural identities have had in a society. Our intent here is not to resolve the challenges of using terms to describe ethnic and racial groups both for specific groups (Latine, Black, Indigenous, etc.) as well as a collective group ("People of Color"). Rather, what we share here is how we are using these terms throughout this text.[2]

---

[2] A particularly helpful guide around language and terminology related to equity and justice issues can be found at Group Health Foundation (2023).

To that end, we will use the following racial/ethnic/cultural descriptors:

- **Black** to refer to all people who have African roots and ancestry including those who define themselves as African American;
- **Latine** to refer to all people of Latin American and Caribbean roots and ancestry who may define themselves as Latina, Latino, or Latinx;
- **Asian American and Pacific Islander** to refer to all people who have roots and ancestry in Asia and the Pacific Islands;
- **Indigenous** (more detail provided below); and
- **Students of Color.** Because we are writing this book to students from a variety of racial and ethnic backgrounds, we use this term to refer to those who self-identify as members of ethnic, cultural, racialized, and minoritized groups.

We use the umbrella term Students of Color to highlight the common forms of oppression, and resistance to that oppression, that still define and describe the experiences of being called "minority" in contemporary society. In doing so, we acknowledge how larger systems of oppression impact so many others who are not in the mainstream—sometimes more accurately called the whitestream (Grande, 2004)—and who may not be reflected or represented in the traditional American construction of racial categories. Most importantly, we communicate a common goal for all those within that umbrella: thriving personally, socially, professionally, financially, and living healthy.

We recognize that this umbrella term might minimize significant differences within and between various racial and ethnic groups. What we realize is that to achieve the aims we hope for, for each group, requires different strategies, support systems, and interventions. That is, we have a common goal for all students even while we acknowledge that each has different needs. This is called **targeted universalism** (powell et al., 2019).

There will be times when we reference a specific racial or ethnic group. It might be when we use a general term like Asian American or a more specific term like Vietnamese American. We prefer the use of these specific categories and use them whenever possible.

While using the term "Students of Color," we acknowledge several other aspects of our identity. For example, Latinos ethnically can also be racially

White, Indigenous, or Black. Black Latinos, for example, often identify as Afro-Latino.

We also know that race and ethnicity intersect with other important aspects of our identities (our gender, sexual orientation, social class, etc.). To honor contemporary requests aimed at gender and sexual neutrality, we use the generic pronoun terms "they" and "their" as often as possible. We will explore some of these "intersections" in other chapters of the book.

Indigenous Students and Students of Color (ISOC)

We will most often use the term **Indigenous Students and Students of Color (ISOC)**. More specifically, we place the words Indigenous Students in front of Students of Color because it speaks to the specific examples of colonization, land theft, and genocide experienced by these nations. It also acknowledges the political and First Peoples status of the thousands of tribes and nations across the Americas.

We understand Indigenous as a primarily political term that recognizes First Peoples and First Nations given the following:

1. *Presence*: They have been historically silenced, marginalized, and made invisible due to centuries of invasion and colonization;
2. *Agency*: They are not passive participants in the politics that affect their lives;
3. *Ongoing Resistance*: They are continuing to struggle against colonization; and
4. *Recognition*: They are aware that borders are human constructs in the service of colonization and alienation.

As such, the term Indigenous is different from a specific tribal name such as Tlingit or Madesi. These tribal affiliations entail a unique and specific language, culture, social system, and history different from the hundreds of other tribes that exist in the Americas and throughout the world. The term *Indian* is a primarily racial term that carries a lot of historical baggage. And *Native American* and *American Indian* are contentious political and racial terms that encompass only the tribes in the United States. While there are nearly 600 tribes in the United States, there are thousands more worldwide that the term *Indigenous* embraces.

OTHER TERMS OF NOTE

We provide a list of some other terms you will see used throughout.

- **postsecondary education:** We use the terms "postsecondary education" and **"higher education"** interchangeably to refer to any education you receive after graduating from high school. When describing it as an "institution" (such as postsecondary institution or higher education institution), we mean the specific organization offering a postsecondary degree. These are general terms that encompass technical school, community college, college, or university levels of higher education.
- **campus:** We use this word to refer to the setting (physical place) of the postsecondary institution, recognizing that some higher education institutions, especially those that primarily use online learning, may not have a physical campus.

Because we frame this book around a cultural wealth, capital, and asset approach to postsecondary education, different from how these are used in the field of economics, we explain the following terminology we will use throughout this book.

- **community cultural wealth:** As used here, the "array of knowledges, skills, abilities, and contacts possessed and used by Communities of Color to survive and resist racism and other forms of oppression" (Yosso & Garcia, 2007, p. 154).
- **cultural capital:** As used here, cultural capital "refers to an accumulation of specific forms of knowledge, skills and abilities that are valued by a particular group" (Yosso, 2005, p. 76) in society.
- **asset:** An asset is a useful or valuable thing, person, or quality. Typically, we think of human assets, institutional assets, physical assets, and cultural assets (Groundwork USA, n.d., para 1).

Introduction

- **cultural assets:** We refer to cultural assets as "the arts, music, language, traditions, stories, and histories that make up a community's identity, character, and customs" (Groundwork USA, n.d., Cultural Assets).

Given these definitions, we use the word "asset" to refer to a specific skill, value, or resource. We use the word "capital" to focus on the accumulation of all the assets that you have in any given category.

We explore these terms more fully in Chapter 2 and throughout the remainder of this book.

We hope you find the reasons for reading this book compelling for you. As you move through the remaining chapters you will find that we add additional terms along the way. The various additions are meant to engage you (and others) as you extend your thinking about what you are reading. We use the terms we do in this book with an understanding that others may use the same or similar words differently. Our intent is to be clear about the terms we use in this text, making it easier for you to navigate and understand the text and easier to use this book as a tool on your path to thriving in higher education.

We are thrilled that you have found your way to this book (however that may have occurred). We are excited to share the wisdom we have gleaned over many years as Indigenous Faculty and Faculty of Color; it has been pivotal to our success and the success of those Indigenous Students and Students of Color we have had the privilege to know.

Most importantly, we hope and trust that this will assist you in your first steps toward thriving in postsecondary education. And it is this thriving that we most hope you will experience. We hope you can be guided in this journey by the words of the inspiring writer and activist Maya Angelou: "My mission in life is not merely to survive, but to thrive; and to do so with some passion, some compassion, some humor, and some style."

TWO

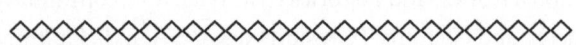

An Assets-Based Approach
Thriving in Postsecondary Education

Five students who are friends and who come from the same racially and ethnically diverse community are beginning their senior year in high school. One warm afternoon they find themselves sitting outside in the school commons talking about the options they are considering after graduation. **Josephine** is fully committed to going to a university out of the state, where other members of their family have gone, to study sociology. **Anna** has a desire to become a registered nurse and she is headed to the local community college, although she aspires to get her 4-year degree. **Teew** is uncertain about what he wants to do and is considering taking a gap year to try to figure it out; for him, just making it into a college may be a challenge. **Kieran,** the son of immigrant parents, wants to go to the local technical school that offers a degree in web design; like Anna, he is curious about whether going on for his bachelor's degree in computer science might be possible. **Pancho** wants to go to a small college in a different part of the state to become a teacher. Anna, Kieran, and Pancho would be the first in their families to extend their education beyond high school.

    The students are nervous, given that this will be a new experience for them. They know little about what postsecondary education will be like and wonder if the schools they might attend will be supportive of them. Each has questions about whether they are fully prepared to be successful. What makes them nervous is different for each: what it will be like to move away from home; how they and their family can afford it; whether they are fully academically prepared; the connection between their field of study and possible work opportunities afterwards.

Rather than thinking of what makes them anxious, Josephine reminds them that they already have lots of experiences and skills that have been helpful for them as they get close to high school graduation. After all, she says, they have attended high school through a pandemic. They have also been part of student walkouts in support of Black Lives Matter and to protest gun violence in schools. Anna points to a book that she's picked up that describes an assets-based approach to thriving in higher education. Teew asks, "What does an asset-based approach even mean?" Kieran suggests that they read it together to see if it helps calm their fears and reduce their anxiety. Pancho, on a recommendation from one of his mentors, suggests that they also consider taking a class this summer at a local community college as one way to learn about college but also to stay connected with each other after graduation.

INTRODUCTION TO AN ASSETS-BASED APPROACH

We write this book for many reasons. Two of the most important are to equip you to realize the dreams you have for yourself while also attending to the dreams others (family members, mentors, community leaders, etc.) have for you after high school. Additionally, we aim to help you see that you can succeed (indeed, thrive) in your formal education in pursuit of your dreams without losing your full and authentic self in the process.

To achieve these goals, we introduce you, as a prospective or current student, to an **assets-based view** to thriving in postsecondary education. An assets-based view is one that focuses on all your strengths and abilities, including how to further develop them and use them to your advantage.

An assets-based approach aims to sharpen your overall view of yourself, promote your sense of well-being, and help you address challenges you may experience in higher education. Beyond its application in school settings, it is also a healthy way to think about and to walk in the world in terms of how you think about yourself and your interactions with others.

> ***Think Alone/Think Together:*** How would you define an assets-based approach to thinking about yourself and your community? What do you already know about assets-based approaches? What questions do you have about those approaches?

We use an assets-based approach to thriving in postsecondary education for two main reasons. First, you might be nervous or anxious about stepping onto a higher education campus, worried about what you have not experienced, or what you have not learned. We want to help you value and affirm the knowledge, experiences, skills, and talents that you do have or that you can access. That is, *you have assets.*

A second reason is that we believe an assets-based approach will be a helpful way to think about what you are learning in classes where you are enrolled. You may hear (or read) ideas in and outside of your classes that seek to minimize or criticize racial, ethnic, gender, or other sociocultural identity groups and communities to which you belong or to which you are connected. We want to prepare you to push back against those ideas especially when directed toward any underrepresented community. One way to do that is to point out that *our communities have assets*. We will now explore these two reasons in greater detail.

YOU HAVE ASSETS

The things that you have yet to learn, experience, or do—recognizing, of course, that all people are continually learning, growing, and developing—can serve to undermine your sense of confidence if you only focus on the things that you lack. A focus on what you do not know, what skills you do not have, and what experiences you have not had reminds you of what and who you are not. This is described as a **deficit-based view**. On the other hand, if you realize that you have already experienced, gained, and learned lots of things that will be helpful to you on your postsecondary education journey, this view of yourself and your abilities will serve you well.

In this book we focus on your assets: your sense of what you are already capable of accomplishing. As these assets are expanded and strengthened, your confidence will grow and success becomes a stronger possibility.

All people bring different assets with them into their postsecondary education. What we highlight in this book are the assets that you already bring, the assets you can access from others, and the unique assets that you are developing because of your particular experiences as Indigenous Students and Students of Color (ISOC). We want you to think of assets as the skills, perspectives, and experiences you and your network have that can help you to be successful in a variety of situations, including in higher education.

For example, if, growing up, you had to learn a new language, dialect, or communication style because of being a newcomer to any new social and cultural community, you possess assets that will help you thrive as you learn new words and language associated with higher education academic topics. This is an example of a linguistic asset.

As another example, if you have felt the sting of prejudice or discrimination and still were successful—perhaps even despite those experiences—you will probably be able to address other instances of prejudice or discrimination that you might experience on campus. This is an example of a resistance asset.

Sometimes, you have these assets and at other times these are assets that you can access. You may find yourself returning to seek the advice and support of a former teacher, a neighbor, a community leader, or a mentor. This is an example of accessing your social assets.

These are just three examples of the kinds of social and cultural experiences that can be best understood as assets unique to ISOC that can serve as a springboard to help you thrive in a postsecondary education setting. Each of these, along with other assets we help you identify in this book, are important in helping you attain your hopes and dreams. Thus, we want you to value and affirm these social and cultural assets as well as all the other individual assets that you bring because of being your unique self.

OUR COMMUNITIES HAVE WEALTH

A second reason we share this assets-based approach is because all too often much of the national narrative—the dominant ways things are defined and described in the media and in public policy debates, by politicians and others—focuses on what our communities lack or what they are not. This is especially true of the ways our social and cultural communities are often described. The national narrative, for example, often frames social problems as the loss of a "traditional" family structure (such as a two-parent, heterosexual household), or the failure to read books to one's children, or the failure to teach children to be independent. Some who hear and believe these dominant national narratives think these best explain why Indigenous People and People of Color and their communities struggle economically, politically, educationally, and in other ways.

> **Think Alone/Think Together:** Provide an example of a time or instance when someone said something that framed your ethnic group in a negative way. What did you think? How did you respond?

Consider, instead, a different version of the dominant narrative. For example, we can describe how these same experiences can serve as positive sources. Think of the skills and values that can be learned from those single-parent role models. Think about how we gain some of the most important wisdom and life lessons not from books but from listening to the stories of our parents and elders. Think about the strength you gain from going to postsecondary education for yourself (independent) but also for your family and community (interdependent). We encourage you to keep an assets-based way of thinking with you as you attend postsecondary education.

We also encourage you to prepare yourself to speak up when conversations demonize your cultural community. Push back against claims about what your community is not (deficit). Part of that preparation includes anticipating the possibility of pushback from your teachers and from other students. The deficit-oriented narratives that so many have heard can be so ingrained in their thinking that it will be hard for them to think differently. We hope you will find ideas throughout this book on how to resist these claims as well as other ideas about how to prepare yourself to speak up.

In sum, rather than take a deficit-based approach to postsecondary education, we urge you to take an assets-based approach to understanding both yourself and your (and other) cultural communities. In doing so, we urge you to value and affirm your sociocultural background as an essential tool for thriving in higher education.

> **PRO TIP:** Use an assets-based approach when thinking about yourself and your community. It's a healthier, more positive, and more affirming way to think about yourself and others.

A NOTE ABOUT THEORY

As we mentioned, one purpose for writing this book is to help you thrive on your postsecondary journey. An important aspect of that success will require you to expand your academic thinking and vocabulary so that you can engage meaningfully with what you are learning. One such concept and word is "theory." There is a strong likelihood that you will encounter theories in almost all your classes. Consider that an assets-based approach is one theoretical lens we ask you to adopt to help you thrive on campus.

> ***Think Alone/Think Together:*** How would you define theory? Why do you think it is important to know what a theory means? In what way are theories operating in your personal life?

Having said this, we want to minimize any anxiety you might have regarding learning about "theories." A **theory** is a "set of knowledges" (Anzaldúa, 1990, p. xxv) that describes how we think something works. As part of our natural growth and development, all people almost instinctively generate and test theories. That is, we each develop and act on our own personal theories.

Consider this simple example. If your cell phone is not working, you begin to develop a personal theory about why it is not working. You might theorize that the battery is dead, or the software system needs to be upgraded, or moisture has gotten into the phone. You then test the theory to see if it is correct or not. You plug the phone in for an electrical charge, you reboot your phone to start up and, if it is still not working, you place it in a dry location for some time before trying to start it once again. All along you have developed a personal theory based on what you know about how personal phones work to see if it explains what you are experiencing.

Academic theories are no different. We develop theories about why some groups of people live below the poverty line, why some groups of people experience greater health disparities, and why some groups of people experience higher incarceration (jail) rates. The theories developed for each of these are attempts to explain how and why something is occurring. We then try to put these theories to the test to see if they help to explain what is occurring.

We also act on these theories even as they are being further developed. For example, if we theorize that some groups of people are more obese than others because they lack proper education about nutrition, the solution would be to create information-sharing activities aimed at teaching about making healthy food choices. On the other hand, if we theorize that obesity is occurring because underserved communities often exist in food deserts (areas with limited or no access to affordable healthy foods as well as culturally appropriate groceries), we might advocate for the development of a local community food cooperative and community garden program.

As these examples suggest, theories impact the way we think about phones—and how we think about our world. At the same time, it is important to understand that our theories are not facts but are "best guesses," which are tested to see how well they explain why and how things work. This, in turn, hopefully creates better guesses and better theories: theories that more closely align with reality *and* help us make a difference in the world.

While theories help you consider how some things work, they can also stop you from considering other ideas that might also provide sound explanations. In the personal phone example, from above, the problem could be many other things, such as a faulty logic board or an inoperable charge cord. In the obesity example, we may not be considering the role of rising food costs, the role of genetics, or the

> **PRO TIP:** Embrace the importance of understanding theories—including being critical of them—that set out to explain how things work. Theories provide a road map of sorts and often can be illuminating around topics and subjects of interest.

lack of affordable physical care available to prevent health challenges while also monitoring overall health and well-being.

DEFICIT-ORIENTED VERSUS ASSET-ORIENTED THEORIES

As we have been explaining, one set of theories that we hope you will join us in challenging are deficit-oriented approaches that focus on what people lack or do wrong. Deficit thinking has been, and still is, used to describe a variety of social inequities. Some of these deficit theories describe social inequities as a result of genetic inferiority, nontraditional family structures, or poor individual and family choices. That is, these sets of theories focus the blame on people by highlighting what they are not.

Deficit theories have been dominant for so long in our society that they seem almost natural. We hope that you will be keenly attuned to deficit orientations when you hear or read about them in classes. As we suggested earlier, we urge you to remain vigilant and wary of any theories that seek to dehumanize any group of people.

We also know that there are some theories that help us to see the world in a more complex, loving, compassionate, and humane way. Rather than focusing on what people are, or are not, these theories urge us to think differently about others by focusing on their assets and the complexity of their experiences. As we detail below, a community cultural assets approach is one such theory.

In using this assets-based approach, we extend our thinking to include both the personal assets that you bring, as well as the assets you have access to in your community in support of your success.

As we are reminded by Anzaldúa (1990), "If we have been gagged and disempowered by theories, we can also be loosened and empowered by theories" (p. xxvi)

CULTURAL CAPITAL: AN ASSETS-BASED APPROACH

One way to think about your assets is to consider them as a form of capital. Consider going to a bank to deposit money; that deposit is your financial capital. The bank is set up to take deposits from you in the form of cash, checks, or electronic transfers. At a different time, you might need to borrow money. The bank looks at your financial capital (past bank statements, current accounts, etc.) to decide if you are trustworthy of a loan. Financial capital is great because it can get you things you want and need that cost money, for instance like buying a car, supporting your family at a time they may be experiencing financial hardship, or traveling abroad.

Note that in this example the bank is not set up to take other kinds of resources (i.e., capital). You might have a strong network of friends and family, a desire to get an education, an ability to overcome hardships, strong motivation to make a difference in the lives of others. These other resources, these other forms of nonfinancial capital, are not considered when applying for a loan. However, these nonfinancial forms of capital can be extremely valuable and helpful to your ability to achieve your hopes and dreams.

So it is with thinking about various forms of capital as assets. Rather than focusing on financial capital, we encourage you to think about the kinds of capital you develop as a member of a particular cultural group; this is your cultural capital. We intend this book to be helpful in this regard.

Our society, like the bank in the example just used, is set up to value some forms of capital more than others. For example, students tend to do well when they demonstrate the kind of capital valued in schools, such as speaking a particular form of English, providing data (facts and figures) to support an argument you make in a paper or speech, and being able to take and complete standardized exams.

Correspondingly, when ISOC cannot, or choose not to, demonstrate White, middle-class forms of capital in schools, the blame is often placed on the students or their cultural group, which others might consider deficient. Working with a group of teachers, one of the authors recalls being told by an elementary school teacher that her students "have no language." The students spoke Spanish, but it was not a form of capital recognized, let alone valued, by that school and that teacher.

Justice-oriented advocates (students, parents, scholars) have pushed schools to consider and value other forms of learning, other forms of capital. This might include allowing other languages and dialects, using personal stories as proof of an idea while speaking and writing, and providing other options for you to demonstrate what you know besides a paper and pencil test such as via a poem, or rap, or drawing. These advocates have also pushed

An Assets-Based Approach

schools to recognize other kinds of knowledge and ways of learning employed in homes and communities of those most marginalized in our society, and this can serve as a connection point to learning.

Consider that every family and child learns important ideas about the world around them. These are termed "funds of knowledge" (Moll et al., 1992). People learn many things from the ethnic and racial communities they come from. Often this knowledge is not recognized in school settings.

The proponents of "funds of knowledge" argue that recognizing and building upon what ISOC do bring in terms of skills, values, and knowledge can assist these children in being successful in schools. For example, think about all the knowledge the child of farmworkers might be learning when listening to their parents talk about weather patterns, soil quality, growing seasons, seed germination, fertilization, as well as advocacy for fair wages and compensation, union organizing, better housing, and more.

> **Think Alone/Think Together:** What kinds of knowledge have you gained from your family that has been important in your life? What knowledge have you gained from your community?

We argue that rather than just focusing on those forms of capital and knowledge valued in schools, we have the opportunity to think about other kinds and forms of capital (i.e., different assets) that ISOC bring in terms of racial and ethnic capital (Solórzano & Delgado Bernal, 2001; Yosso, 2005, 2013, among many others) that are essential to your success even if these forms of capital are not valued by schools.

As one more example, consider the following extended passage about what it means for a child, prior to entering kindergarten, to have "basic skills" (a kind of capital valued in schools) and to be "ready to learn."

> If we're going to ensure that all children learn to read, I believe we have to turn our notion of "basic skills" on its head. What we call basic skills are only "basic" because they are one aspect of the cultural capital of the middle class.
>
> What we call advanced or higher-order skills—analyzing new information, evaluating the relative merits of concepts and other problem-solving

skills—are those that middle-class children learn later in life. But many children from low-income families learn them much earlier because their parents place a high value on independence and real-life problem-solving skills.

So children come to us having learned different things in their 4–5 years at home, prior to formal schooling. For those who come to us knowing how to count to 100 and to read, we need to teach them problem solving and how to tie their shoes. And for those who already know how to clean up spilled paint, tie their shoes, prepare meals and comfort a crying sibling, we need to make sure that we teach them the school knowledge that they haven't learned at home (Delpit, 2014, pp. 18–19).

COMMUNITY CULTURAL WEALTH

Let's go deeper with the assets-based approach we are advocating for you to adopt for yourself and carry with you in your academic pocket. We do so by describing community cultural wealth theory (Yosso, 2005, 2013). It is this framework that guides the rest of this book and organizes the chapters you will be reading. Recall, from Chapter 1, our definition of community cultural wealth as the accumulation of all forms/kinds of cultural capital held by a particular social and cultural identity group to survive and resist experiences with racism and oppression (Yosso & Garcia, 2007).

We have continually heard educators complain that Indigenous Parents and Parents of Color do not care about their children's education. They may not have gone to their child's school on parents night, participated in family "fun" nights, or attended Parent-Teacher-Association (PTA) meetings. Of course, you can imagine the many reasons why they may not have attended these school events. Transportation challenges, child-care needs, working evenings, lack of translation services, their own negative school experiences—many things may explain why they do not come to the school. Note that none of these has anything to do with how much these parents care about their child's education.

One such Scholar of Color, Tara Yosso (2005), to counter the claim that Parents of Color do not value their children's education, interviewed Latine parents about the ways they and the broader cultural community do in fact support the education of their children. Parents described the ways that they do, in fact, support their children's education but in ways not usually accounted for or valued by schools. In essence, this scholar was trying to uncover the specific and unique forms of Latine cultural capital, spread throughout the community, that show they value education.

These forms of cultural capital, adapted from Yosso's work and described by Cuauhtin (2019a) include: Aspirational, Familial, Linguistic, Navigational, Social, and Resistance Capital.

- *Aspirational Capital*: "The ability to maintain hopes and dreams for the future even in the face of real or perceived barriers" (p. 247).
- *Familial Capital*: "The cultural knowledge nurtured among *familia* (kin) that carries a sense of community history, memory, and cultural intuition" (p. 248).
- *Linguistic Capital*: "The intellectual and social skills learned through communication experiences in more than one language and/or style" (p. 248).
- *Navigational Capital*: "The skills of maneuvering through social institutions" (p. 249) such as banks, businesses, government agencies, and others so that needs can be addressed and met.
- *Social Capital*: The "networks of people and community resources" (p. 248) one relies upon, including adults and teachers.
- *Resistance Capital*: Those "knowledges and skills fostered through oppositional behavior that challenges inequality" (p. 249) and strives for social justice.

Since the publication of this initial work, others have added to this list as they identified other kinds of capital that make up community cultural wealth. Here we summarize some of those additional forms of capital as described by Cuauhtin (2019a).

- *Political Capital*: How "people and communities influence power and decision-makers" (p. 249) along with other forms of political action to exert power for change.
- *Ancestral Capital*: "The roots of one's ancestral legacy, one's ancestral funds of knowledge," (p. 250) talents, and ways of being that come from one's ancestors especially before colonization.

- *Ecological Capital:* The "relational knowledge about nature, the environment, and all ecology" (p. 250), wherein people connect to and see themselves interdependent on the land and the environment.
- *Discursive Capital:* "The actual doing of community cultural wealth" (p. 250) in ways where you share and apply your cultural knowledge and the specific skills of well-being in ways that foster action.
- *Spiritual Capital:* The sense of hope and faith ... rooted in a connection to a reality greater than oneself (Galván, 2006).

For our part, we identify and explore two other forms of capital that make up community cultural wealth not included in these lists. We advance the idea of cultural capital and **humanizing capital**. We offer that cultural capital, while certainly inclusive of these other forms of capital just described, is a unique asset. Thus, we adopt the following definition of cultural capital.

> *Cultural Capital:* Those things valued by a group or community that contributes to the identity and unity of that group or community (Stern, 2022, What is a Cultural Asset?). It includes the specific forms of knowledge, skills, and abilities that are valued by a particular group (Yosso, 2005). This cultural capital is made evident when used with your discursive capital.

We advocate for the idea of humanizing capital as another resource that can assist you on your higher education journey. To that end, we offer the following definition.

> *Humanizing Capital:* "The process of becoming more fully human as social, historical, thinking, communicating, transformative, creative persons who participate in and with the world" (del Carmen Salazar, 2013, p. 126).

Think Alone/Think Together: As you read these forms of capital, what strikes you as interesting? Which do you want to know more about? Which of these do you see as already an important part of your life?

Our intention is to significantly extend and enhance your own *navigational capital* to increase your chances for success in postsecondary education. Our aim is to help you to recognize that you do not come to higher education as empty containers waiting to be filled with knowledge and skills to be developed. Rather, we want you to see, understand, and then rely on your own personal and community cultural wealth (capital) as a primary way to support your success in postsecondary education.

In relying on these forms of capital, and the specific assets that they contain, we hope that you are beginning to recognize that you do NOT have to give up your heritages—the community cultural wealth you have and have access to—to succeed. Rather, we hope that you will come to see how your community cultural wealth can and will play an essential role toward success on a college campus.

We believe that you, as a prospective or postsecondary student, will find this a strong framework that, in and of itself, will be helpful to you both personally as well as academically. It bears repeating that we want you to use this framework to assist you in your coursework, both in terms of class participation and in completing assignments. It also bears repeating that, beyond its application in postsecondary settings, it is also a healthy way to think about life and walk in the world.

USING COMMUNITY CULTURAL WEALTH TO ORGANIZE THIS BOOK: AN OVERVIEW OF WHAT'S TO COME

As we have suggested, we aim to foster an understanding of how your Community Cultural Wealth—that is, the various forms of capital and assets—are central resources for your own success in postsecondary education. We only focus on the following forms of capital, including combining a couple, in the following chapters: aspirational, cultural (and ancestral), linguistic, familial and social, political and resistance, navigational, and humanizing.

In each chapter, we describe what these forms of capital are, how you can identify them, and ways to develop and strengthen them. We then make connections to each of these forms of capital and their implications for what you might experience on your college campus; that is, we explore how the assets in each of these forms of capital can be helpful to you. We also identify some "pitfalls and caveats," things to watch out for and be careful about, related to each of these forms of capital. Within each of these chapters is general advice for success for ISOCs in postsecondary education.

In sum, we use an adapted version of community cultural wealth (Cuauhtin, 2019a; Yosso, 2005) to organize the contents of this book. We hope that seeing and exploring more deeply most (but not all) of these specific forms of community cultural wealth will help you to see that many of the assets you bring to postsecondary schooling will support your overall academic success and help you to thrive once admitted.

In **Chapter Three** we ask you, as a prospective or postsecondary student, to ponder your grandest hopes and dreams as an approach to uncovering your own aspirational capital and that of your communities. One way we will do this is to introduce ourselves to you and share some of our own aspirations, first as ISOCs ourselves and now as Indigenous Faculty/Adminstrators and Faculty/Administrators of Color. More specifically, we share our own grandest hopes and dreams when we were students, like yourself. We share a moment of joy in our own education journeys and our hopes for you. We will share some questions we have asked ourselves about what it means to thrive in higher education settings, questions you may have for yourself. We will then provide a broad overview of some initial things to consider as you prepare for your postsecondary journey.

In **Chapter Four** we discuss cultural (and ancestral) capital and how you can apply this capital in higher education. Using descriptions of cultural and ancestral capital (Cuauhtin, 2019a), we examine how you, as an ISOC, can recognize and rely on your own cultural capital to not only foster well-being on campus, but to thrive in positive ways. We want you to be able to advocate for yourself personally and on academic matters as a result of seeing you have cultural assets. We hope you come to understand that you can share your cultural assets to educate others, choosing when, and whether, to reveal these cultural assets. We also take time to discuss the nature of oppression and how it operates to undermine your cultural and ancestral identity and capital.

In **Chapter Five** we extend the conversation about cultural capital to focus on your linguistic capital. Given the relationship between language and culture, we identify a variety of ways you can understand language(s) as an asset. We include, in linguistic capital, dialects and communication styles as equally important. Beyond helping you to identify your linguistic capital, we also identify ways to deepen and strengthen these important assets.

In **Chapter Six** we will discuss how you, as an ISOC, can connect with the network of people and community resources—your familial and social capital—to help nurture and support you throughout your postsecondary experience. These are networks that have supported you, up to this point, and nurtured you. However, many students leave their families and communities when they go on to higher education to attend schools out of state or in a different region within the state. What is important to understand is that there are some new networks in postsecondary settings that are also committed to nurturing your growth and success. Some of these networks (such as academic advisors, financial aid officers, counselors, etc.) are available to all students while others are specifically committed to assuring the success of ISOC students. Finding these networks, familiarizing yourself, and making use of them when appropriate will go a long way to assuring you thrive in higher education.

In **Chapter Seven** we focus on political and resistance capital. We think this is a particularly important form of capital as you come to recognize that education is a political activity. That is, the decisions about what you are being taught, how it is being taught, and how what you are learning is being assessed, among many other considerations, are all political decisions that encourage you to conform to societal expectations—or encourage you to walk toward broader freedom and liberation for you and your home community. As you develop your own critical and political consciousness, a central aim for most in postsecondary settings, you will begin to see how oppression works against you (personally) and your home community (culturally). Being able to understand this provides ample opportunity for you to develop your skills associated with resisting forms of oppression on both the personal and social/community level.

In **Chapter Eight** we create a direct and explicit focus on navigational capital. We expect that you will have identified the significant assets that you bring to postsecondary settings by the time you get to this chapter. Thus, in this chapter we will turn our attention to the ways ISOCs can successfully navigate postsecondary institutions. We will discuss how postsecondary institutions are organized so that you can maximize what they have to offer, which will enhance your success.

In **Chapter Nine** we delve more deeply into humanizing capital, which we have added to the list of different forms of capital (Cuauhtin, 2019a; del Carmen Salazar, 2013; Yosso, 2005) identified so far. Earlier in this chapter, we described humanizing capital as the ways in which you see yourself not just as a student but as a human being with broader hopes and needs (beyond schooling) who desires a connection to others and the broader world. Who you are, in its most broad sense, is also a central part of your success in postsecondary education, a theme we hope you are gleaning thus far. We hope you will seek out and take advantage of opportunities to develop your physical, artistic, social, and spiritual self. We do this because we recognize that attending to these other aspects of yourself will be central to your well-being as well as your physical and mental health while on campus.

In the **Conclusion**, we ask that you "put it all together" to maximize your potential to thrive in postsecondary settings. The focus in this conclusion is to reiterate the importance of taking the tools offered in the text, practicing and applying them, in order to thrive and flourish in institutions of postsecondary educational settings. We come back to our grandest hopes: that the book helps you find your most authentic self and realize your aspirations and potential.

We include in this book, at the end, an open letter to Faculty, Staff, and Advisors about how they can support the ISOC students they encounter. We also have developed a Glossary of Terms used in the book to assure that you can access the ideas we provide throughout this book.

> ***Think Alone/Think Together:*** As you read this description of the chapters to come, what questions does it raise for you? What are you most looking forward to learning more about? Why would that be important to learn more about?

An Assets-Based Approach

We are so glad you found your way to this book. We write it with the grandest hopes that you will find your postsecondary experience one that opens new vistas, deepens your understanding of the world of possibilities, and provides the foundation for a life that is purposeful and meaningful. We believe all this is possible when you identify and use the many assets that you already bring as well as deepen and extend others. It is your capital—the assets you bring and develop—that most make possible our goal for you: to not only survive but to thrive in postsecondary education.

At the same time, we encourage you to consider how these forms of capital and assets—both those that you identify as current strengths and those that you are deepening and developing—will serve you beyond your schooling experience. We also believe these assets carry over into how you live "in a good way," where you see yourself, and everyone around you, as a promise. That is, we are confident that seeing and affirming the assets you bring will serve you well, not just in postsecondary education, but in life.

U.S. Poet Laureate Joy Harjo (a member of the Mvskoke Nation), in *Crazy Brave* (2013), reminds us of the importance of using these assets, these gifts, to lift you in countless ways: "If you do not answer the noise and urgency of your gifts, they will turn on you. Or drag you down with their immense sadness of being abandoned."

THREE

Aspirational Capital
Pursuing Your Dreams

In early spring of their senior year, the five friends decide to attend a lunchtime talk provided at their school as part of the school's "Exploring Careers" series. The speaker is a graduate from their high school who not only earned her college degree but also her medical degree. The doctor is well known in the community because she provides health treatment and advice at a local health center.
She surprises the five friends by sharing that she too had fears and concerns like those they had previously articulated to each other. The speaker also shares that she went to college for more than just earning a postsecondary degree. What kept her going, she related, was her desire to give back to the community that supported her efforts.

    Afterwards the five students go out for pizza. Their conversation turns to each sharing their own hopes and dreams for the future. Josephine talks about how getting a postsecondary degree will be a stepping stone to a bigger dream: becoming a professor someday. Anna says she wants a nursing degree, so she, like the speaker, can help improve the health of others. Teew says he'll be happy just getting a degree, since he will be the first in his nuclear and extended family to go to college. Kieran wants to get a degree doing something that he loves but that will also enable him to get a job so he can help support his family. Pancho wants to teach at their local middle school. Like the speaker, he hopes to be able to give back to their community.

Aspirational Capital

> ***Think Alone/Think Together:*** What are your dreams for your future? What/who has influenced your dreams? What do you want to be when you grow up?

INTRODUCTION TO ASPIRATIONAL CAPITAL

In preschool and kindergarten, teachers often ask their young students, "What do you want to be when you grow up?" Students are asked to share their dreams of becoming a basketball player, doctor, police officer, or teacher. Sometimes, they are asked to draw pictures of what they want to be when they become adults. Teachers praise students for dreaming of their future careers.

This assignment is a common and popular exercise in schools across the country. What they do not tell kids at that moment is what they will need in their invisible toolbox to attain that goal.

Of course, basic skills are taught in public education around "reading, writing, and math" and sometimes critical thinking. These all go into a student's invisible toolbox. But we know it takes much more to achieve a dream.

For Indigenous Students and Students of Color (ISOC), teachers leave out the part about the barriers that will stand in their way as they struggle to navigate the world to attain their goals. For some, the dream they envisioned as a child becomes less and less possible as they grow older. Dismal, we know. However, this book—as you have read in the introduction—is about making sure your dreams, whether the ones you had as a young child or the ones you are dreaming of now, can come true.

EXPLORING ASPIRATIONAL CAPITAL

Aspirational capital is about hope, resiliency, strength, support, perseverance, and aspiring to reach your goals. Acquiring aspirational capital is about "dream[ing] of possibilities beyond [your] present circumstances, often without the objective means to attain those goals" (Yosso, 2005, p 78).

In other words, you may not have all the tools yet to achieve your dreams. We ask you to keep dreaming and to know that there are lots of people who will help you get there.

Stories from our families of struggle and overcoming barriers are what nurture each of us to dream of what the possibilities might be for our future. Sometimes it is the dreams and aspirations of our families for us. At other times, it is our own dreams that motivate us to reach for the seemingly impossible. Aspirational capital is about returning to the "why" that started you, and us, on the path toward reaching for our dreams and finding a way through the barriers.

This chapter asks you to ponder your grandest hopes and dreams as a method of discussing aspirational capital. We will introduce ourselves and discuss our positionality—where we come from, who we are, and how we arrived at the place we are at presently—as Faculty of Color, what our grandest hopes and dreams are for you as ISOCs, and a moment of joy in our own education.

Each of us, the authors, has a unique story to share about our educational journey. We all come from different backgrounds: ethnic groups, socioeconomic status; we differ in age, gender, and family structures. Our paths through postsecondary education vary, and our abilities vary, but the journeys we have been on to get us where we are today intersect in ways that we hope will help you navigate through postsecondary institutions to reach your goals.

As you travel toward your goal, things will sometimes feel uncertain. The "why" we do things in life is important to remember and return to when you are questioning the path forward. Come back to "why" you are choosing postsecondary education in the first place.

Remind yourself of the reasons you started on this journey. Maybe it was for yourself, to achieve what you believe will be fulfilling and make you happy. Maybe your "why" is your family or your culture or both. The "why" for you might be about giving back to your community, to the next generation, or to make a change in the world for a more just and democratic society. It might be all the above, and that is okay too.

Sometimes the "why" you started out with in the beginning may not line up with a shift in your goals as you have new experiences or are influenced by what you are learning. It is natural to re-evaluate your goals and modify your "why." Life is fluid, and learning to bend with the flow will support you when you question your path forward. Returning to your "whys" will ground you in your resolve and motivate you to push past the barriers or roadblocks toward your goals. Remember: *You got this!*

INTRODUCTION TO THE AUTHORS

Each of us, the authors, has come to where we are today by navigating through the maze of obstacles in our paths toward our goals in postsecondary education. We are diverse scholars from diverse personal, cultural, professional, and academic backgrounds. Together we represent the fields of law, English, education, Native American and Indigenous studies, Black studies, Latine studies, Asian American/Pacific Islander studies, and gender and women's Studies. We have all occupied roles as teachers, professors, and administrators in postsecondary education.

We come from diverse Communities of Color where going to college was not a common pathway, nor did we often feel our cultural backgrounds were acknowledged or even accepted (let alone affirmed) as a valid grounding for success in postsecondary education. We intend for you, the reader, to get to know us a bit and hopefully find commonalities in our journeys that affirm your own journey. Thus, we each provide a glimpse of some of our most important experiences. We each share at least one moment of joy during our college experience. We end each of our narratives with our hopes for you since these served as a central purpose in writing this book. We present these narratives in alphabetical order.

Dr. Jacquelyn Bridgeman

I was fortunate to grow up in a family that highly valued education in general, and higher education in particular. By the time I got ready to go to college I was the fourth generation to attend college on my mother's side and the second generation on my father's side. Something unlikely in most families, but nearly unheard of in an African American family.

Both of my biological parents earned their bachelor's degrees (they met in college) and both went back and earned advanced degrees later in life. In fact, my mother went back to school to earn her PhD in psychology the same year I started college. My maternal grandfather was a medical doctor (internist) and my maternal grandmother held advanced degrees in chemistry and physics. My maternal great-grandfather was a dentist, and my great-grandmother was the first Black social worker in the state of Mississippi.

Between my biological parents and my stepparents, I have 12 aunts and uncles. All but three of them have college degrees. My paternal grandfather was not able to attend college, but he worked tirelessly in the steel mills in Indiana and extra jobs on the side in order to help pay for his younger siblings to attend college and to make sure all of his children earned college degrees (which each of them did). Accordingly, for me, whether I was going to college was never a question. The question was which college I would go to.

I was born in Denver, CO, and then my family moved to Wyoming for the first time when I was six because of a promotion my father received from work. Less than 2 years later we moved back to Denver, and 3 short months after that we moved back to Wyoming when my parents divorced.

The small-town community in Laramie, WY, proved to be a good place for my Mom to raise kids as a single mother. As a result, I spent the 1st through 12th grades in schools where I was often the only Black kid in the entire school and where sometimes there might be fewer than 50 Students of Color in a school of nearly a thousand. Predominantly white would be an understatement. I attended schools and lived in a part of the country that was almost exclusively White.

I excelled in school, likely due in no small part to the value my family placed on education and the way they always supported the same. For as long as I can remember I loved school. I loved reading, I loved learning new things, I loved challenging myself. And I enjoyed schoolwork. I was also a very good athlete.

I often think one of the most defining moments of my life happened when I was in 1st grade. From the moment I knew what reading was, I wanted to learn how to read. So, when I got into 1st grade it took almost no time for me to learn how to read and to become one of the best readers in the class. We had two carts full of reading books in my 1st-grade class: one for bright kids who could read, and one for struggling students. Despite the fact I could read well, my 1st-grade teacher limited me to the books at the bottom of the cart for kids who couldn't read. It didn't take me long to figure out, even as a 6-year-old, that my placement at the bottom of that cart had nothing to do with my ability and everything to do with being the only Student of Color in my entire class. My response was to read every single book on the cart for lower kids so she would have no choice but to move me up where I belonged.

Unfortunately, the experience I had in 1st grade would be one of many such experiences I would have throughout my K–12 education. And each time it happened, my response was largely the same: work harder, be better. On the one hand, racism and sexism pushed me to achieve and set me up to attend some of the best schools in the country, but it also made me feel like I was in a constant fight most of my life.

Until I went to college.

For college, I deliberately picked a school that not only valued diversity but prided itself on supporting students from diverse backgrounds. For the first time in my life, not only was I not the only one; I was surrounded by supportive students and faculty members who assumed I would achieve, and who supported me in doing so.

My moment of joy started the spring of my sophomore year when I attended a guest lecture put on by a woman who studied African American communities throughout the Americas. Until that time, I had never known there were so many Black people throughout the world. I hadn't known that so many did not have the same history of slavery and the same degree of oppression that I had known in the United States.

That lecture turned into a research project on African maroon societies (descendants of enclaves of escaped slaves who lived in freedom) in Ecuador—a research project funded fully by a grant I received from the Stanford Anthropology Department, and a project that resulted in my graduating with honors and choosing to pursue a degree in Anthropology and African American studies (two disciplines I had never heard of until I went to college).

The work I did in Ecuador helped me to understand myself as an African American woman and my connections to the broader African **diaspora** (the movement of people away from their ancestral homelands) in ways that were life changing. That first research project, and the thesis I wrote because of it, helped me get into law school, and has influenced all my research since. It helped me better understand my place in the world and my value as a human being.

My hope is that this book will help you take advantage of the wonderful experiences and learning opportunities that higher education provides. Opportunities that can be as positively transforming as my college experience was for me. I hope you will then take your success and experience and use it to produce good for others in the world, whether that be in your local community, region, or beyond.

Dr. Angela M. Jaime

I was born in Yreka, CA, close to my mother's homeland and tribal community. The Pit River Tribe is located on the northeastern side of Mt. Shasta and includes eleven Bands; mine is the Madesi. I was raised by a single mother who finished high school, went to one semester of college, met her future husband, and became pregnant with me before her college dream could be realized. She was my inspiration as I navigated through postsecondary education.

During my 11th-grade year, all my peers were preparing to apply to colleges and deciding what they wanted to do after graduation. I followed suit to the school counselor's office to inquire about the standardized test prep course needed to prepare for the exam. She poured over my grades from the past 3 years and turned to me to say, "Have you thought about cosmetology school? The community college has a great program. You style your hair so nicely, so you'll do great. Then you won't have to take the test." I was 17 and very self-conscious of my academic skills, so I shrugged and said I would check it out.

When I shared this with my mom that evening, I could tell she was unhappy. She made a visit to the school the next day, and by lunchtime, I was enrolled in the prep course. My mom might not have had the academic capital to navigate the postsecondary landscape, but she was surely not going to let anyone discourage her daughter from going to college. I learned a lot of valuable lessons from my mom while I was growing up and watching her advocate for me. She is a strong woman; that she passed down to me.

I was an athlete in high school, and that skill took me to Santa Rosa, CA. Santa Rosa Junior College (SRJC) had on-campus dorms and provided me with support while I played sports. I reconnected with my Indigenous culture through student groups, Indigenous professors, safe spaces on campus established for Students of Color, and my teammates.

I transferred to California State University, Sacramento, after 2 years at SRJC to pursue my bachelor's degree. I really did not know what I wanted to do with my life. There were so many choices, but I limited myself to degrees that did not have math or science requirements. I was a struggling student in high school, and my first few years in college with these subjects were no different. I could not see myself being successful in any field that required me to calculate numbers or compounds.

I changed my major six times before deciding on ethnic studies with a concentration in Native American studies. I realized late in my undergraduate degree journey that studying and performing well in college was about repetition, regurgitation, and who you know. It took me 5 years to finish my degree. During my journey, I encountered a few faculty who supported me and helped me navigate the system.

A moment of joy for me in postsecondary education was when my Indigenous professor during my first semester in SRJC asked me to stay after class and recognized that I was Indigenous. It affirmed to me that I belonged. I looked at her and saw a part of myself reflected back. Dr. Brenda Collins supported me throughout my postsecondary education journey. She also wrote me letters of recommendation for entrance to all three universities I attended. She advocated for me on countless scholarship applications. She planted the seed of success I carry with me to this day. I hope to be that same kind of support for other Indigenous students for as long as I am able.

My hope for you, the reader, is that you reach out to those educators who offer you support and who help you navigate the system. Seek out the student support services on campus managed by People of Color and spend time with them. Let them get to know you; this will make it easier for them to advocate for you as you work toward your dreams and goals. Ask lots of questions, and do not be too proud or afraid to ask for help. We all need guidance and advocates. There is nothing we do alone.

Dr. Francisco Rios

I was raised, primarily, on Denver's West side, which was dominated by the Latino/Chicano community. I grew up during the height of the Civil Rights Movement, though the Chicano Movement was gaining strength.

My father's parents, my grandparents, were from Mexico. My mother's family was from northern New Mexico. They had lived there before New Mexico became a part of the United States. As my grandmother (and many others) claimed, "we did not come to the United States; the United States came to us."

I did not even consider going to college as I grew into my teens. I imagined that, after high school graduation, I would get a job in a factory, buy a car, get married, and settle down. That was what had occurred for almost everyone in my family. I thought that would be my story too.

In 11th grade, a Cuban American teacher named John Vidal asked me to stay after class. He said he thought I had potential and that I should think about going to college. It was the first time I ever considered the possibility. He helped me to develop some literacy skills, encouraged me to apply to Upward Bound (a college-preparation program), and talked to my parents about the importance of higher education.

I was the first in my immediate and extended family to go to college. At one point I almost quit. I recall my Tia Ramona telling me that I had to be successful because I needed to model what was possible for our family and community. That advice kept me going.

A moment of joy for me was the first time I received straight As in college. I had never received these in high school. This was especially surprising given that I was not fully prepared for higher education. But I had lots of help along the way, especially since I lacked some important academic skills (writing, most notably). An English professor told me that my (lack of) academic preparation did NOT equal my academic potential. This lifted me in ways that would stay with me throughout my profession/career.

I am most hopeful that you will find a way, in all that you do, to keep those from your family and community at the forefront of your actions and beliefs. They are often the people who most believe in you, who are sacrificing so you can go to college, and who need to know from you who we in our cultural communities can become.

Dr. Kevin Roxas

My father and mother immigrated from the Philippines more than 60 years ago now. What I always thought was interesting about my father was that whenever he was in public settings (like on a bus or at the store) and he saw somebody he thought was also Filipino, he'd say "Pare ka ba?" The translation of this phrase in Tagalog is, "Are you a friend?"

If the person was Filipino and spoke Tagalog (the national language of the Philippines), the person would respond in Tagalog or in English and inevitably the conversation would continue from there about where they both were from in the Philippines, who else they knew from the Philippines in the city where they now both lived, and often an exchange of phone numbers and the promise of catching up and meeting up at a later date.

When I was a kid, my siblings and I used to always dread my father asking literal strangers if they were friends. We doubted whether he would ever know anybody to whom he asked this question. When I look back, though, I realize that asking this question of people he met in public places was important for him because he was using this opening question as a meaningful way for him to connect with other immigrants presumably like him from the Philippines. It was, I think, a way for him to initiate a possible friendship, and a way for him to feel connected and grounded to other Filipino immigrants in an area where he didn't know a lot of people. In other words, he wasn't literally asking if these strangers were friends. In his own way, he was asking if they could be his friends and supporters in a country he wasn't born in or fully connected to.

My father's (and mother's) experiences as immigrants in the United States impacted me throughout my childhood, my time in school, and my time in college. Having attended predominantly White schools, I did not have the opportunity to have a Teacher of Color throughout my kindergarten through high school years. Even in college, I only had two professors in total who I remember connecting with students from diverse cultural groups in ways that, at the time, seemed meaningful and supportive. These experiences in school and college seemed to create both physical and psychological distance from my own personal experiences growing up in a family and home community of Filipino immigrants.

While my parents spoke Tagalog at home, no one at school ever asked me about it. While my mother was a tremendous cook of delicious Filipino food (and food from other cultures), the only time this was highlighted at school was once a year at the International Night at my elementary school. While my family was part of a larger trend of immigration of Filipino immigrants to the city of Chicago and across the United States, the stories of my parents, my aunties and uncles, and others that were playing a part of a larger Filipino diaspora across the world were not included as part of the curriculum, discussion, and lifeblood of the schools I attended.

After graduating from high school, I eventually ended up going to a university about 2 hours from my hometown. One of the joys I experienced at my university was when my mother would come to visit me. She would bring Filipino food for me that she had likely prepared for days and would also take me and my roommates out for a meal (or two).

She really enjoyed meeting people I had gotten to know through school and hearing more about what the college experience was like. In turn, my friends and roommates enjoyed meeting and knowing her, learning about her and our family story, and connecting back to her.

The joy I experienced from these visits had multiple sources: Joy from seeing my mom whenever I experienced homesickness. Joy from seeing my mom have a chance to share parts of herself and our family story with my friends. Joy from seeing her being a part of my college experience, an experience she and my father had worked so hard to provide.

For readers of this book, my hope is that you will always remember the ways in which members of your families and home communities have supported you throughout your life and provided you with the skills and determination to be successful as you start your postsecondary education. Always remember that you have key people in your life who are rooting for you to be successful and who want you to thrive.

Making sure you remain connected to these people and firmly grounded in the strengths that your family and home communities bring to new spaces you enter in postsecondary education is one important way of feeling supported and successfully navigating postsecondary education.

Dr. Caskey Russell

I am from Seattle, WA, and spent my entire life until the age of 30 in the Pacific Northwest (PNW). I never thought I'd leave the PNW, but after dropping out of college and spending a few years as a musician, I returned to the university and made it my career.

I moved to the Midwest, to the mountain west, and eventually, after many years away, I returned to the PNW. I mention this because I see my life as one ongoing (and often contradictory) mixture of elements. My life embodies a mix of races, geographies, urban and rural settings, class sentiments, and attachments, and it has taken a long time to become comfortable with a mixed life.

My mother's family is Tlingit, which is an Alaskan Native tribe. My father's family is White. With my mother's side of the family, I got to hear the Tlingit language, learn about the culture, and partake in the foods and traditions of my Tlingit ancestors. My Tlingit relatives were also civil rights leaders and activists in Alaska. I heard stories at an early age of their bravery and how they fought for Indigenous rights in Alaska. My mother's family held a strong sense of pride in Tlingit identity and a different narrative of history than what I learned in grade school and high school.

My father's family was from Aberdeen, WA (home of the grunge group Nirvana). They were Irish and German settlers, devout Catholics, whose main occupation was roofing. In the rainy climes of the PNW, roofing is usually steady work, but my father's father had a debilitating drinking problem that forced my father to grow up in a difficult environment deep in poverty. My father's family held a strong sense of class anger and a mistrust of institutions except for the church and the military.

My parents met in Seattle, but unfortunately, their families disliked each other. *Utterly* disliked each other. I can't recall the two sides of my family ever gathering together. They had to be kept apart to avoid violence: my grandfathers famously got into a drunken fistfight on my parents' wedding night. The two other times they met ended in fights as well.

As I've grown older, I realize that I've spent much of my personal and intellectual life trying to find peace with the mixture of my life—trying to symbolically bring my two families together in my mind in a way that never happened in real life.

This is why the university has been a vital force in my life: The university has been a place of stability for me since I was a student and often provided a supportive environment as I explored my identity and connected my personal life with my academic goals. My time within the university has allowed me to understand this mixture, understand its racial and geographical underpinnings, and ultimately find a workable peace in living the mixture.

I find true joy in working with Students of Color and helping them thrive and succeed in higher education. My hope for you, the reader, is that this book can help you navigate the challenges and the joys that you'll find in postsecondary education. Your success at the university, college, or community college is like creating an initial path through the thick, ferny forests of the Pacific Northwest: Every time you succeed, you make the path more visible. Your success clears the path of obstacles and turns what was once impassable into a well-worn road that can be more easily navigated each time by those who come after you.

> ***Think Together/Think Alone:*** What are your initial reactions to these narratives? What stands out for you? What lessons can you take away? What questions or cautions do they raise for you? What story would you tell?

Having shared a little about our stories and our trajectories, we now turn to those things we wished we had known prior to entering our respective postsecondary institutions. Some of us wondered about the different kinds of universities and colleges, as well as the types of degrees you can earn there. Some of us wondered about the advantages and disadvantages of living at home versus living on campus. A question each of us wondered was how to access financial aid and other forms of assistance.

CAREER CHOICES AND CHOOSING A MAJOR

Think back to the beginning of the chapter where we described how teachers ask young students (and presumably, you) what they/you wanted to be when they/you grew up. Your answers as a child and your answers now might be similar or completely different. Either way, given your postsecondary education journey, you will be thinking about what career you will want to have and that means in terms of choosing a major or field of study.

There are several resources available to help you choose a career path. There are aptitude and interest inventory tests given to secondary students

Aspirational Capital

across the country. Career service centers on high school and college campuses often can provide you with literature about the career options and how to channel your passions into a future path.

One thing to think about when choosing a possible career path is the career choices of people in your life. Sometimes we follow the path of those around us. This makes for easy access to someone in the profession you can ask questions of—someone who will be able to give you the dos and don'ts when pursuing that career.

For career paths that you may not have a network of people to draw from, consider summer **internships** and volunteer opportunities while you are still in high school. These hands-on experiences can provide you the chance to see careers and the environment in which you would be working. These opportunities are also available at the postsecondary institutions you might attend as well.

Having an idea of the major or career path you are interested in can help you make decisions about the universities or colleges you might choose to apply to attend. Later in the chapter we will talk about the choices you will need to make regarding how to choose a university or college to apply to and which one will be the best fit for you.

TYPES OF COLLEGES AND UNIVERSITIES

Once you have decided that you want to continue your education beyond high school, you will need to consider the type of postsecondary institution you will want to attend. Technical colleges often have a focus on preparing students for a specific career and often have more workforce-specific approaches to classes they offer. Sometimes the credits earned in technical colleges can count toward a diploma and sometimes they can count toward a 2-year or 4-year degree.

We provide an overview, in Figure 3.1, of the types of degrees you might pursue and how long they might take if you attend full-time. Please understand that many factors may speed up the amount of time required (for example, taking summer classes) or slow the amount of time required (for example, changing majors or skipping a quarter/semester).

Figure 3.1. Types of Degrees and Typical Time to Completion

Abbreviation of Degree	Degree Title	Undergraduate or Graduate	Years to Completion
AA	Associate of Arts	Undergraduate degree	2 years
AS	Associate of Science	Undergraduate degree	2 years
BA	Bachelor of Arts	Undergraduate degree	4 years
BS	Bachelor of Science	Undergraduate degree	4 years
BFA	Bachelor of Fine Arts	Undergraduate degree	4 years
MA	Master of Arts	Graduate degree	2 years beyond a bachelor's degree
MS	Master of Science	Graduate degree	2 years beyond a bachelor's degree
MFA	Master of Fine Arts	Graduate degree	2 years beyond a bachelor's degree
DEd	Doctor of Education	Graduate degree	4 years beyond a master's degree
PhD	Doctor of Philosophy	Graduate degree	4 years beyond a master's degree
JD	Juris Doctor (law degree)	Graduate degree	3 years beyond a bachelor's degree
MD	Doctor of Medicine	Graduate degree	4 to 10 years beyond a bachelor's degree

Community and junior colleges usually teach the first 2 years of undergraduate study and award degrees known as associate degrees. Both offer 2-year associate degrees, courses designed for students who want to transfer to a 4-year university for bachelor's degrees, or technical or vocational education training to prepare students for the workforce or careers.

Less numerous are those postsecondary institutions that have a specialization such as the performing arts, automotive training, or military-focused schooling.

> **PRO TIP:** No matter what degree path you choose, there will always be a path toward multiple options for 2- and 4-year degrees. The journey is what you determine is the right path for you. Meet often with your advisor to get the most informed advice on completion of your degree(s).

Other colleges and universities award 4-year degrees known as bachelor's degrees.

A general rule of thumb, but not always the case everywhere, is that institutions with the word *college* in their name are smaller and often focus on undergraduate education, which is an education that leads to 2-year and 4-year degrees.

Since universities can be so large, they often contain *colleges* within them, as is the case with the University of Oregon (UofO). UofO, at the time of writing this chapter, contains 5 colleges and 3 schools: College of Arts and Sciences; College of Business; College of Design; College of Education; Honors College; School of Journalism and Communication; School of Music and Dance; and School of Law.

Each college usually contains multiple departments, and those departments offer majors and degrees. The departments in a university's college are usually grouped in ways that make sense academically. For instance, a university's college of arts and sciences may have departments of art, English, history, biology, chemistry, and psychology—all of which offer degrees in either the arts or sciences. Colleges of business or colleges of education will contain departments related to business and education and offer degrees in those fields.

One additional note about universities. These often offer advanced programs aimed at professional degrees (teaching license, for example), master's degrees, or doctoral degrees.

It is also good to know how institutions are funded: privately or publicly. The difference between a privately funded university and a publicly funded university is the way in which an institution receives a significant amount of money that allows it to pay for the professors, student services, buildings, and events. Private funding comes from student tuition and endowments or donors. Publicly funded institutions rely on student tuition and government funding, both state and federal, and donors and endowments as well.

Ethnicity-specific colleges offer campus environments that are intended to support specific groups of students. Historically Black Colleges and Universities (HBCUs) were established as early as 1839, and the last ones were created after the Civil Rights Act of 1964. HBCUs generally work toward creating academic and cultural environments tailored to Black students' success. HBCUs generally offer undergraduate and graduate degrees.

Tribally Controlled Colleges and Universities were created to provide Indigenous communities equal access to postsecondary education. Their course offerings meet the needs of the Indigenous communities they serve and incorporate cultural practices and teachings specific to the needs of Indigenous peoples.

Hispanic Serving Institutions (HSIs) have at least 25% of their student population identifying as Latine. Minority Serving Universities (MSIs) are created to meet the unique needs of students from diverse backgrounds and are often located in remote areas or urban settings.

> **PRO TIP:** Choosing a school that supports your identity/membership group can make it more likely your college experience will provide a safe and ethnically/racially affirming space for you. It can also open doors to networking opportunities for future employment or graduate degree support.

Researching to find postsecondary institutions to attend that offer the areas of study you are interested in, or activities you find appealing, is time well spent. The degrees available for you to pursue will be determined by the postsecondary institution you choose. Researching your possible career path and the postsecondary institution with the support services you are looking for in your college experience will help you make the right decision for you.

PLANNING FOR YOUR FUTURE BY CHOOSING THE RIGHT INSTITUTION FOR YOU

If you are in your final years of high school or finishing up at a community college, choosing your next steps will require gathering information and researching the institutions you would like to attend. There are a variety of postsecondary institutions that will help you fulfill your aspirations.

Internet research and asking questions of those you know who have attended a college or university you want to know more about can help you choose the right postsecondary institution. Many colleges and universities have a special "Future Student" or "Prospective Student" tab on their homepages. Some have videos of students speaking about their experience, what attracted them to the institution, and advice for new students. This section of the website might also have information on special activities offered, the size of the campus population, class sizes, programs they offer, and more.

These websites most often also include virtual campus tours and provide information on in-person visits. We encourage you to sign up for the campus tours and visit multiple campuses if you are able to learn as much as you can about schools in which you have an interest. Data on who attends the institution (breakdown by ethnic groups, age groups most prevalent in the first year, student enrollment by academic major, etc.) and an ethnic breakdown of the faculty can be found on the website in the "about" tab for the institution.

These websites will share information about the town surrounding the university or college, transportation to and from the town (airports, trains, buses, etc.), and access to amenities. Explore the websites of the schools you are interested in as much as you can. Then start asking questions when you cannot find the information you are seeking.

One thing to search for is if the postsecondary institution does *direct admissions*. Direct admissions are like being pre-approved for a credit card. You haven't applied for the credit card but based on your credit score companies have offered you pre-approval. For direct admissions, students post their profile (including grades, interests, test scores, etc.) on approved websites that offer this service and partner with universities. Colleges and universities use this information to offer an immediate admission to their university without the student having to fill out all the application paperwork and wait for replies.

PRO TIP: Look for schools to apply to that might have direct admissions based on your GPA or test scores or both. These early direct admissions opportunities allow you to be admitted in the first rounds of admissions, freeing you to use your time to apply to other schools whose applications might require more time.

Location

One important thing to consider when doing your research on postsecondary institutions is the location. *Are you considering living at home?* Depending on where you live, you might have access to a college or university or both within the city limits or your home state. In this case, you will have access to campus tours, career counselors, and alumni you can question about the institution.

If you are looking at institutions out of your home state one thing to consider will be the cost of tuition for out-of-state students. This tuition cost is often considerably more than paying in-state tuition. However, sometimes there are agreements between states to offer out-of-state students in-state tuition waivers or scholarships. There are also many tuition reciprocity agreements between states and regions (Midwest agreements, New England agreements, Southern Agreements, Western Agreements, etc.).

Living at home has many financial advantages. The cost of living for students staying at home is considerably less. For most students who live at home, their largest expense will be the in-state tuition and fees. Living at home will not only cut your costs toward college but is an excellent way to draw from the support system of your family while you embark on your first few years of postsecondary education. Many students choose to live at home and commute to college to save money and find their way through a challenging change in their lives. Later in the chapter, we will talk about budget and financial support. In later chapters, we will discuss the resources and support services available to help you feel connected and to foster your success.

To live on or off campus, that is the question.

If you will be living on campus or in the surrounding areas of campus, you will want to search the university website for tabs on student housing. Most institutions have housing support services for both on- and off-campus living that will help you navigate choosing an on-campus dormitory, roommate selection, meal plans, and activities offered to help create community.

Some universities offer learning communities or interest group living options. These options allow students to work in groups with others who have similar interests and experiences. For instance, there may be whole floors in a dormitory for just Indigenous students or students who are engineering majors or who have social justice interests. If you are an athlete, you might live in the same vicinity as your teammates.

Choosing to live on campus can create opportunities for new relationships, networking, and student support through the residential life office in your building or on your campus. Some students enjoy their residential experience so much they take jobs in the later years of their college experience as a residential assistant or floor manager. These positions often offer free room and board as well as a paycheck. Relationships you make at college through campus living, activities, employment, classes, and your major become lifelong connections that will help you in your social life and career path(s).

READY TO APPLY?

The websites of each institution you are interested in applying to will have tabs or special pages for new or future students, which are especially important when you are ready to apply to the postsecondary institution(s) you choose. Often, the admissions criteria and application are located on these pages or within the prompts for new students designed to help you prepare to submit your application packet. You will find instructions on how to apply and what documents you must submit.

Typically, institutions will require you to submit an online application rather than a paper application. These applications will require your personal contact information, your transcripts from the high school you attended and any college you might have taken classes from during your secondary experience, such as Advanced Placement or concurrent enrollment college courses.

The application will also require you to have your scores from standardized tests (SAT or ACT or PSAT), and letters of recommendation from teachers, coaches, or community organizations you belonged to or volunteered for, or from other people who are in a good position to speak to your character and your ability to succeed. Usually those who write your letters will need to send them directly to the places where you apply.

We encourage you to be thoughtful and considerate when asking people to write letters of recommendation for you. The people you ask might be quite busy and have many letters to write. Try to pick people who know you well, can speak to your strengths, and care about your success. Even if they know you, there are likely things about you they may not be aware of that would be important for them to include in their letters. Finally, be sure to

> **PRO TIP:** To make it easier, at least a month before you need the letter sent, if not sooner, ask whether an individual is willing and able to write a letter recommending you. Ask what materials they will need from you to create a recommendation. Offer to have a conversation with them about your hopes and dreams and why you want to pursue a postsecondary education. The easier you make the process for them, the better the letter they are likely to write to help you get admitted to the school of your choice.

thank them. A short, handwritten note, or a kind email are good ways to thank people for their letters.

Standardized Tests

The standardized tests required for entrance to many postsecondary institutions provide additional information about prospective students to the admissions teams. One of the reasons postsecondary institutions require standardized test scores is that grade point averages (GPA) across the country vary, and a GPA is not always a fair indicator of a student's ability to learn or perform in the classroom. Test scores help balance the overall picture of a student's application.

That said, the authors acknowledge the bias of standardized tests; some of us have been victims of these cultural biases. Cultural bias in testing is where tests are designed, whether intentionally or not, with a bias toward dominant cultural predictors (Rosales & Walker, 2021). These serve to limit the success rate of Students of Color and those from low-income families. These tests favor the predominantly White population and those of higher socioeconomic status and cause exclusion of Indigenous Students and Students of Color, especially into prestigious postsecondary institutions. Planning ahead to take the tests during your junior year of high school (grade 11) or the summer before your senior year (grade 12) allows you to have the scores sent to the institutions of your choice or time to retake the tests for higher scores if you need to.

Another reason to take standardized tests is they may help you qualify for scholarships that are awarded based on your test scores or sometimes based on a combination of your test scores and GPA. The PSAT is the only standardized test that qualifies students for the National Merit Scholarship Program. This program offers a National Merit scholarship of $2500 and eligibility for many corporate-sponsored and college-sponsored merit scholarships.

Postsecondary institutions do not use the PSAT to make college entrance decisions, but taking the PSAT will not only provide you the opportunity to be considered for scholarships, but will alert postsecondary institutions to your interest in college more generally. Many postsecondary institutions use the PSAT to connect with students who may be a good fit for their institutions. The PSAT is not a required test, but it may provide you with some financial aid opportunities and help you learn about schools that you might not otherwise consider.

> **PRO TIP:** Take advantage of the ACT/SAT prep courses your high school might offer or the scholarships available to pay for the fee of taking one of these courses. The many ACT/SAT handbooks available (both in paperback and online) with prep materials and practice tests will be essential in helping you prepare.

SAT and ACT tests scores are used to help evaluate academic readiness and comprise one of *many* pieces of a student's college application. Remember, these scores are not the only determining factor in gaining entrance to any institution. A low score does not determine your access to the college or university you most want to attend. Do not let these tests and the score you receive define you. You have so much more to offer the world than just one score.

Writing the Application Essay

Some institutions will ask students to write an essay as part of the application process. These essays are an average of 400–600 words and ask students to share an experience and a bit about themselves. It is one of the many pieces of information the institution collects to make informed decisions about whether to accept a student, wait-list them, or deny their application.

> **PRO TIP:** Your essay is a time for you to share more about your life, the challenges you have faced, and your family. Be your unique and amazing self. Do not merely write what you think the admissions officer would want to hear. It might be a challenge or feel uncomfortable but try to be vulnerable—open up about your past, your hopes, and your dreams.

When writing these essays, talk about the experiences that have influenced your life journey; talk about your culture and family; and share a part of you so the reader sees you as a person and not just an applicant. This essay is an opportunity for you to share with the reader what is not apparent about you in your GPA, test scores, and other general information collected in the application forms, and to provide information that may be missing from your letters of recommendation.

In some cases, the institution you are applying to might ask you to write an essay using a question they provide. If so, be sure to answer the question they ask.

For any application essay you write, make sure you have one or two people who can read it and provide you with feedback on your essay before submission.

We encourage you to use the personal essay in the application to focus on the ways your ethnicity and race have contributed to or defined your journey toward strength, courage, and resiliency. Embrace who you are, your identity as Indigenous Students and Students of Color and how your culture has made you stronger. This essay affirms who you are and how you were raised. Be true to who you are; be your authentic self in the content of your essay. You have something unique and special to offer to any school you might attend. Let them know what that is.

PULLING THE APPLICATION TOGETHER

Do not wait until the last minute. Apply as soon as you can so that you stand out in the pile. Your experience is unique, and you want to stand out. Most schools get a flood of applications right at the deadline. The earlier you apply, the less likely you are to be lost in that flood.

Aspirational Capital

Preparing Your Documents

Here's a list of documents (but not exhaustive) you will need for most applications to postsecondary institutions:

- Transcripts from your high school and any postsecondary institution you have previously attended.
- PSAT/SAT/ACT scores sent to your chosen institution(s).
- Letter(s) of recommendation that speak to your character, what kind of student you are in the classroom and outside the classroom, extracurricular activities you participated in, for example volunteer work and athletics.

Find out before you apply how to order transcripts from your schools (high schools, community colleges, etc.) and what you will need to provide the registrar so the transcripts are sent to the right location.

Once you have located the information you need to apply for admission, explore the websites of the schools you intend to apply to see if the institution requires an application fee. Whether you are applying to one institution or several, these admission charges can be costly and always require you to use a credit card.

FINANCIAL PLANNING

The research and planning that goes into choosing an institution is the first step to picking a university or college that is right for you. Many students think they should not apply to a certain postsecondary institution because the cost is too high, and they cannot afford to attend. Use the application fee waiver and apply to every postsecondary institution you remotely

> **PRO TIP:** There is also a service called the Common Application (available at www.commonapp.org), which is accepted by more than 1,000 schools, including some colleges outside the United States. It helps streamline an essential part of the admissions process for students. Through this service, first-time and transfer applicants can apply to multiple colleges at once.

> **PRO TIP:** Most postsecondary institutions offer application fee waivers for students meeting certain criteria (ethnic background, family income, etc.). Ask about them, apply for them, accept them if offered. There is no honor in denying yourself the opportunity to apply to the institution(s) you want to attend because you were too proud to accept the waiver. Indigenous People and People of Color advocated for these waivers for you to use them. Fee waivers are a resource that is there to support students and remove financial barriers to applying to postsecondary institutions.

want to attend. Do not limit your possibilities. Reach for the stars and apply to them all; the worst thing they will say is no. By not applying you are closing the door. You might apply to 10 schools and get into five. Once they have chosen you, you now have choices on where you want to attend.

Calculating the cost of tuition, student fees, books for each term/semester, living expenses (whether that be living on or off campus), and all personal expenses (e.g., mobile phone, clothing, etc.) is difficult. There are several online resources available to help you prepare for the responsibility of budgeting for your college experience and monthly budget management. In this section, we will highlight some aspects we feel need more attention when pulling together your financial plan.

Free Application for Federal Student Aid (FAFSA)

Preparing for the financial responsibility of paying for your college experience will need to be part of your planning in the early stages. The Free Application for Federal Student Aid (FAFSA) (available at: https://studentaid.gov/h/apply-for-aid/fafsa) determines your eligibility for college-related financial assistance and is available to everyone on October 1st each year and due by February 1st to be eligible for all sources of funding.

The FAFSA will also determine if you are eligible for work-study positions on campus. These work-study positions are paid for by a federal program and provide additional opportunities for experience and funding.

Aspirational Capital

> **PRO TIP:** Develop a budget plan and work with your parents, a counselor, or your friends to determine what will be needed to pay for your postsecondary experience. Do not get discouraged by the costs. There are many scholarships available and need-based financial options to support these costs.

The FAFSA form is required to be filled out by every student who is seeking financial assistance to attend any postsecondary institution. This form requires you to provide information from your parents' tax returns and other information about the financial status of your family (if you are a dependent) or your financial status if you are independent from your parent(s) or guardian(s) for 12 months or more.

The FAFSA will also provide you with your eligibility for student loans (unsubsidized, subsidized, direct PLUS). Subsidized loans do not accrue interest if you are a half-time or full-time student. Pay attention to the interest rate of the loan once you must start to pay it back. These rates can be high and cause financial hardship once you begin the payment plan. Unsubsidized loans accrue interest while you are in school, but you will not have to start the payment process until you are out of school. Credit-based loans will require you to begin paying them back as soon as you accept them; they will accrue interest for the duration of the life of the loan.

Do your research about each loan type before accepting them. Accepting a loan should be the last financial option and you will need to develop a plan to repay the loan.

Credit Card Scams and Debt

Once you reach an age where you have opened a savings and checking account, you will begin receiving credit card applications. The opportunity to apply for your

> **PRO TIP:** The FAFSA will determine your financial aid eligibility for funding for federal, state and local grants, and scholarships. This form is important; do not wait to fill it out. Begin filling it out and submit the forms BEFORE the February 1st deadline to be eligible for all the opportunities you qualify to receive. If you wait, you lose out.

own credit card and charge the things you want will be enticing. Resist the urge to use the credit card. While it is important to have a credit card to build your credit history and credit score, it is also important to try to make sure you pay off the full balance every month.

The trick to good credit card management is to use it only in an emergency or with a calculated plan to pay off the debt immediately each time you use the card. Being fiscally responsible will benefit you later in life when you are ready to buy a car or a house. The debt college students accumulate, and often default on paying back, impacts many opportunities they may have in the future.

Saving your summer money and graduation cash will be important for the months when you might be a little short or have unexpected expenses (medical, car-related, travel, etc.). Make sure you are budgeting your monthly expenses to cover your needs and using your savings in emergency times. There might be a time or two when you will need to make a choice about using the credit card or going into debt by taking out a loan. There is no shame in going into debt when there is an emergency, but having a plan will be essential. Do your research, plan out how you will pay it back, exhaust all options before making the decision to take out a loan.

This chapter has been focused on the empowerment of hopes and dreams. We are encouraging you to embrace your dreams and hopes for your future. Use the inspirations you have in your life to help guide and motivate you toward your goals and future career.

We encourage you to prepare for your journey. Do your research on the schools you are considering and the communities where the schools are located. Prepare for your financial needs and start collecting the documentation you will need to submit to schools. We share a little about our stories with the hope you feel less alone and recognize that others have faced similar, if not the same, challenges.

Your life experiences, your hopes, and those of your community have not only prepared you to follow your dreams but will sustain you along the way. Yet, you won't know what you can achieve until you try. Go for what you want and do not be afraid to seek and accept help along your journey.

More often than not, the difference between those who succeed and those who do not is as simple as who is committed to trying.

At the end of the day, pursuing a postsecondary education is about pursuing the dreams you have for the life you want. In this, we hear the words of former President Barack Obama, "Change will not come if we wait for some other person or if we wait for some other time. We are the ones we've been waiting for. We are the change that we seek" (Obama, 2008).

END OF CHAPTER ACTIVITY: DRAFT AND WRITE THE APPLICATION ESSAY

Practice writing your application essay. When writing your essay, remember to be your authentic self. Share your personal story to provide the admissions officer insight into you and your dreams. This is the time to be open and honest about your past and what you want for your future.

Here are some helpful prompts to consider for writing your essay:

- What words would you use to define yourself?
- What are the most important parts of who you are as an individual?
- What are the most important parts of your social identity?
- Why and how are these important to you?
- What experiences have you had that have helped shape you into the person you are today?
- Reflect on a time when you had an experience that changed the way you see the world or yourself.
- What one thing would you most want the admissions officer to know about you after reading your essay?

When you have completed two of these essays, share them with a mentor. Ask for their feedback and suggestions about how you are describing yourself and your aspirations.

FOUR

Cultural (and Ancestral) Capital
Being Your Authentic Self

Two weeks after their high school graduation, the five friends decide to enroll together in a class at the local community college. Pancho's mentor had recommended taking a summer community college course as a good way to prepare for postsecondary education. The friends agree to enroll in a course titled "Introduction to Ethnic Studies." They have heard good things about the interdisciplinary nature of the class: It focused on history, anthropology, psychology, sociology, and other subjects through the lens of ethnic studies. They have also heard good things about the teacher, a Professor of Color, and thought the class would help them better understand their own backgrounds, each other's backgrounds, and deepen their understanding of the history and contemporary challenges of their own multicultural community.

In one interactive lecture early in the course, the professor focuses on the role of identity in people's lives. The professor explains that we all live and learn from within our identities. While the professor acknowledges that each of us has many facets to our identities, given that the course focus is ethnic studies within the United States, she encourages students to focus on their cultural and linguistic identities. She mentions how important it is for Students of Color to be proud of who they are, and that this will serve them well in school and beyond. For their first written assignment, the professor asks the students to answer the question: Who am I as a cultural person?

Josephine encourages the friends to stay for a few minutes after class to discuss what they have been learning, but also to talk through the question posed by the professor. Each of the students takes a turn discussing how they first came to see their identities, what their cultural

Cultural (and Ancestral) Capital

and linguistic identity means in their lives, and how those aspects of their identity connect them to others.

- Josephine says she is one of very few students and people in their community from her African American social identity group; it was her family that was the primary source of her cultural development.
- Anna describes her cultural identity as an Indigenous person but says that an important aspect of that identity is being a woman. She describes, in particular, what it means to be an Indigenous woman.
- Teew says that he's not thought too much about his mixed cultural identity and has only recently been working to understand it more fully.
- Kieran says that, like Josephine, he is one of only a few people from his racial group in the community but his parents and extended family members, as well as the local Filipino cultural center, help keep this identity vibrant.
- Pancho says he feels very immersed in the local cultural community, which has been growing increasingly in Latine people. He shares his pride in his ethnic and cultural roots.

After sharing, Teew asks the friends, "Is it really true that knowing, understanding, and honoring our cultural identities will be a key to our future success as the Professor says?"

INTRODUCTION TO CULTURAL (AND ANCESTRAL) CAPITAL

Take a moment to think about your identity. Your identity is evident when you think of answering the question: Who Am I? How you answer this question is important because it shapes how you feel about yourself, how you interact with others, and where and how you engage with the world.

In many areas, including education, it has become apparent that your identity matters when it comes to learning. You will engage with postsecondary education differently if you think you are smart versus not so smart.

Similarly, you will engage with academic content, say a math class, differently if you see yourself as a strong mathematician in training versus if you see yourself as weak in that content area. In short, you will behave differently given the different ways you think about who you are as a student.

Our culture (and language, as we describe in Chapter 5) is one important part of our overall identity. We certainly have many parts, and combinations of parts, that make up our **individual identity** that are unique to each of us (funny, good at playing guitar, swimmer, etc.). We also know that a significant part of our identity is made up of features that we share with others. These are our **social identities**. They include things such as our race, ethnicity, gender and gender expression, sexual orientation, class, and religion.

We come to see and understand ourselves in relation to the social identity characteristics we share with others. It is these shared characteristics that often give us meaning and purpose. That is, we learn from others who share a common social identity with us what it means, for example, to be "Laotian" or "female" or "Muslim" or "Native Spanish-speaker."

What is more, it is often these shared or social parts of our identities that most people notice first. Not only do they notice these parts of our social identity first, but they begin to make judgments about what kind of person we most likely are as a result.

> ***Think Alone/Think Together:*** As we have described the role of identity as a key part of who you are, what are the 3–5 top descriptors of your personal identity? What are the 3–5 most important parts of your social (shared) identity?

In this chapter, we discuss and describe what it means to have cultural capital and how you can apply cultural capital assets in postsecondary settings.

EXPLORING CULTURAL CAPITAL

In Chapter 1 (Introduction), we described cultural community capital as the collection of assets—skills, values, and knowledge—gained from your cultural social identity group that can assist you in being successful. More specifically, a community's cultural assets are those things "of value to a particular population, community, or group because of its unique contribution to the cultural, artistic, creative, economic, historic, and/or social expressions and fabric of that community" (Stern, 2022, What is a Cultural Asset?).

A community's cultural assets can be tangible, such as a heritage site or things produced by that community, for example murals depicting the people who live there. The community's cultural assets are also intangible and might include "events, activities, expertise, support networks, community and cultural knowledge, and heritage, language, organizations, and icons" (Stern, 2022, What is a Cultural Asset?).

It is both the tangible and intangible community cultural assets that shape the kind of experience, knowledge, and wisdom that you might have gained. Recognizing and highlighting these community cultural assets shows that the communities to which you belong have value and are valuable. Community cultural assets help members feel successful, adaptable, and unified. It is also these assets that push against negative (deficit) descriptions of a cultural community and, instead, show that the cultural community is deserving of respect and justice.

In discussing cultural and ancestral capital (Cuauhtin, 2019a) we encourage you as Indigenous Students and Students of Color (ISOC) to recognize and rely upon your assets. They will not only help foster your well-being; they will help you thrive in postsecondary education. Given this, we want you, as a prospective or current postsecondary student, to be able to advocate for yourself personally and academically as a result of seeing that you have cultural assets.

Sociocultural Identity

To understand and then affirm these assets, we delve more deeply into your cultural identities. We help you gain this understanding by exploring, more broadly, your social identities related specifically around race and ethnicity. That is, we explore your **sociocultural identity**.

You are probably aware that our social identities, particularly around race and ethnicity, are more than just labels we use to describe who we are.

Our social identities have broader meanings and implications related to power and powerlessness. Some social identity groups have greater social power, oftentimes using that power to marginalize other groups.

Given historical and contemporary society in the United States, when it comes to race and ethnicity, White (in terms of race) and Eurocentric (in terms of ethnicity) social identity groups hold greater power in our society. This power gives those groups the opportunity to create the conditions in our society under which we live. This includes the power to structure how social institutions (banks, courts, schools, elections, etc.) work most often in ways that maintain the power and status of the dominant group. At the same time, other social identity groups have been and are less socially powerful in the mainstream, with less opportunity to shape or change social institutions or even know how these social institutions work.

> ***Think Alone/Think Together:*** What parts of your identity do you feel are most affirmed at home? At school? In work settings? What parts of your identity do you feel are less valued at home? At school? In work settings?

Despite this, we want you to see how your cultural identities are assets, whether society sees them as such or not. These assets serve as a foundation to push against (that is, resist) the conditions that work against you and your community; they also enable you to thrive because you see yourself and your community as a promise. The key to thriving in your identity is to be able to self-define, to determine for yourself how you want your identity defined, and to tell the world how you should be defined. We must define ourselves or we will be defined by others (Szasz, 1973).

Understanding Culture

To understand more fully what we mean by cultural capital and sociocultural identity, we need to understand what we mean by "culture." *Culture* can be a difficult concept to understand. Broadly speaking, *culture* is defined as "the norms, values, patterns, of communication, language, laws, customs, and meanings shared by a group of people located in a given time and place" (Sensoy & DiAngelo, 2017, p. 36). It includes "the set of practices that keep a society together and allow its members to find meaning in their lives" (Baldock, 2010, p. 2).

Schools, institutions, and nations all have cultures specific to their locations, citizens, employees, student bodies, and laws. While it is valuable to consider all these other uses of the term culture, of importance to this book is the understanding of sociocultural identity: We are interested in those aspects of your identity that you share with those from your common racial and/or ethnic affiliation.

Grasping fully what culture is can also be complicated because it operates on different levels (Sensoy & DiAngelo, 2017). On one level, the surface culture, are those things that you can readily observe, for example what people prefer to eat or how they eat it, how they dress, or how they celebrate special occasions.

On another level are those aspects of culture that operate just below first awareness or impression but are evident with keen observation. For example, you might observe individuals who, when interacting in a work setting, spend much of their time focused on relationship building. Or you might observe others who do very little in terms of relationship building and, instead, get right to the tasks at hand. You might conclude that the first group of individuals operates within a "relational orientation" while those in the second group take a more "task orientation." The orientation one adopts may be culturally influenced.

Finally, there are aspects of culture that are nearly invisible, such as what people from a particular sociocultural identity group value or how people make sense of or understand the world as a result of being part of a shared culture. In fact, sometimes even people within a particular ethnic or racial group are not even aware of these deeper influences of culture on their lives.

Consider, for example, why people from some groups put candles on birthday cake or shake hands when greeting others. When asked "why" they do this, they may simply say "it's just what we do," without knowing the underlying reasons or value orientations around why these traditions were adopted in the first place. In short, because the most important parts of

Figure 4.1. Iceberg Model of Culture

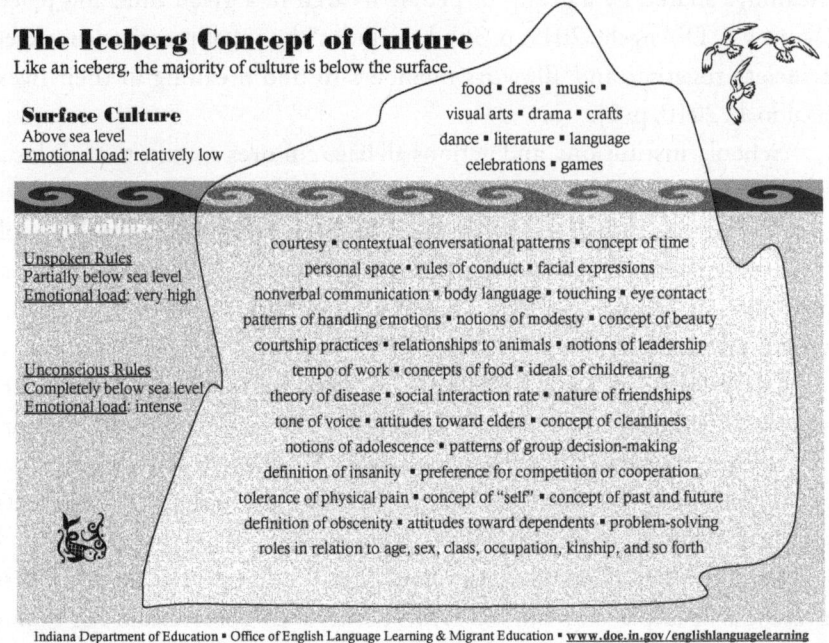

Used with permission of Indiana Department of Education.

culture lay at these deep levels, defining and describing a people's culture is challenging even for those from that cultural group.

A visual that is helpful is the iceberg model of culture, adopted from Hall (1976), which shows the varying levels of culture and their elements (see Figure 4.1). Viewing culture within an iceberg metaphor is helpful in that the biggest and often the most important elements of culture lay below the surface.

Race and Ethnicity

Within this broad understanding of culture are two other forms of identity—race and ethnicity—that are a primary focus of this book and, we believe, are also likely very important to you. We recognize that there are other important aspects of social identity (such as class, gender, nationality, etc.) but discussing these are beyond the focus of this book.

Race is typically thought of as a system for classifying people based on physical features (called *phenotype*) such as skin color, hair features, and bone structure. This classification did not merely seek to understand differences but included attempts to place value judgments (i.e., better-worse, stronger-weaker, capable-incapable) on these differences. This classification system was then used to explain and, in the United States to justify, discriminatory actions. That is, we know race is a social, cultural, and political concept that has been used, historically and contemporarily, to justify oppression.

Ethnicity is used to describe the bonds people share based on language, traditions, and ancestry. Different from race, which is a classification system imposed on others to oppress, ethnicity is most often self-defined.

When thinking about racial and ethnic identity, it is important to understand that our identities are multiple, fluid, contextual, and strategic. We have more than one identity that is important to our views and perceptions of who we are (*multiple*). While someone may be Puerto Rican ethnically, they also have a race, class, and gender identity to name just a few markers of identity. These identities can and do change over time (*fluid*), though sometimes very slowly. What it meant to be Black or Indigenous in the 1960s is different from what it means to have those identities today. Certain identities play out differently in some settings than in other settings (*contextual*). For instance, you may identify, or be identified, as a Student of Color when interning at a cross-racial community center, but when attending a local Powwow you may identify as an Indigenous person. Finally, when and how we share certain parts of our identities, and which ones we choose not to share, is often purposeful (*strategic*). For example, when questioned by immigration officers, your identity as an "American" may be the one you emphasize more than your identity as a speaker of the Tagalog language.

> ***Think Alone/Think Together:*** What words would you use to define yourself? What are the most important parts of who you are as an individual? What are the most important parts of your social identity? Why and how are these important to you?

A CAUTION ABOUT CULTURE, RACE, AND ETHNICITY

As suggested earlier, coming to an accurate understanding about culture (and race and ethnicity, by extension) is difficult because, among other things, it is changing (dynamic) and responsive to the specific setting in which it is operating. With respect to its dynamic and evolving nature, we are especially aware that young people, in particular, adapt their cultural practices, values, and worldviews to the contemporary moment.

With respect to operating in specific settings, we are aware that culture is responsive to the conditions where they are located. How Mexican American culture is experienced, for example, is different in East Los Angeles, than it is in Topeka, KS, or New York City. Culture is influenced by the unique setting in which it is situated.

The caution, then, is to push against those who make sweeping generalizations (referred to as *essentializing*) about any particular sociocultural identity group as if that culture, race, or ethnicity can be described as a specific set of traits. Rather, see culture as locally specific. Even individuals find ways to use those parts of the entirety of their cultural, racial, and ethnic toolkits to live in ways that make sense to them within those local settings.

Instead, work to affirm the notion of a **cultural community** defined as "a coordinated group of people with some traditions and understandings in common, extending across several generations . . . and continual change among the participants as well as transformation of the community's practices" (Gutiérrez & Rogoff, 2003, p. 21). That is, when exploring any culture (including your own), ask how it is experienced and expressed differently based on locale, generation, and individual levels.

> ***Think Alone/Think Together:*** Have you had an experience where someone made a sweeping (essentializing) generalization about your cultural community or some other cultural community? How did you feel? What did you think? How did you respond? Is there anything you would do differently?

A NOTE ABOUT INTERSECTIONALITY

Every person has multiple social identities. While you may have a specific racial and ethnic identity (such as Afro-Latino), you may have a gender identity, a religious identity, a refugee/immigration identity, and so forth.

What is essential to know is that sometimes these identities intersect in meaningful and important ways because each of these has differing levels of power. These intersections impact who has access to opportunities (privilege) versus who is excluded or limited in those opportunities (oppression). For example, a Latino may be limited in opportunities because of his ethnicity but, because of his gender, granted more opportunities than a Latina.

Scholars of Color, particularly Black female scholars, have been on the forefront of thinking (theorizing) about these interconnected and overlapping identities. They have named this focus on multiple identities and their relationship to power as **intersectionality**. They have called out how these various dimensions of identity (say, for example, being a Latina) can create interconnected and compounding forms of oppression. These are more than just two separate forms of oppression; together they are a new form of oppression.

An intersectionality lens requires us to be mindful to go beyond thinking of ourselves and others as having just a racial and/or ethnic identity. An intersectional lens helps us to understand that while some parts of our identity might not be privileged (for example, being Vietnamese), other parts of our identity might be privileged (for example, also being male and **cisgendered**). We hope it also spurs you to understand other forms of oppression (such as gender, religion, economic class, citizenship status) and engage in ally building across these differences.

What is important to know is that we see intersectionality as an asset. It allows you to bring multiple (and interconnected) ways of thinking about the world with you wherever you are, including on a postsecondary campus. While it often creates greater complexity, it also represents the real tangible and concrete ways in which people live and regard themselves. A person who focuses only on one part of their identity (say ethnicity) loses out on sharing the many other important contributions they could make based on their collection of identities. In short, we see intersectionality as another valuable kind of cultural asset.

> **Think Alone/Think Together:** Given what you have learned about culture and what we have described in this text, how would you define culture in your own words? What would you say if you were to describe the importance of your culture to a friend or fellow student?

A key task for you, as a postsecondary student, is to understand the relationship you have between your own individual identity and various social identities, including those based on race and ethnicity (sociocultural identity), as you proceed into and through your postsecondary education experiences.

HONORING YOUR CULTURAL ASSETS

Your learning can be enhanced when you come to both understand and embrace your cultural assets. Based on how we described culture in this chapter, we hope you can see how your cultural assets help you to think about the world in more than one way. This spurs greater creativity and greater flexibility in the ways you make sense of what you are learning. We assert that your own cultural knowledges will add to your perspective on what you are learning, thereby deepening an understanding of the world of ideas from which you can learn.

> **PRO TIP:** Consider classes in the field of anthropology if you find yourself interested in learning more about culture generally. These courses delve more deeply into what we mean by culture generally and provide an opportunity to learn all the different ways in which culture (and being human) plays out.

Your schooling experience was more than just an activity that happened in your head. Learning took place with others (teachers, other students, staff, etc.) and within particular cultural value systems. Given your cultural identities, and your success in school, you have probably also learned how to learn and be successful in new settings as well as how to navigate the cultural ways of being that are important in those settings.

Specifically with respect to culture, except for identity-affiliated institutions such as a Historically Black College or University, a Tribally Controlled University, or a Hispanic Serving Institution as described in Chapter 3, most postsecondary schools have centered and continue to center the needs and experiences of White Euro-American male students. While attending these institutions, you will need to strengthen your skills associated with understanding and navigating those cultural norms.

More specifically, given that you have already been successful in K–12 schools, you have already learned how to cross cultural borders associated with learning. Postsecondary education is not different in this respect. You will be required to adapt to new (even if not totally unfamiliar) cultural frames associated with postsecondary schooling and even within academic disciplines. In essence, you have already learned how to cross cultural borders associated with learning even if you have never left the United States.

At the same time, we want you to be mindful that these new cultural orientations and languages that you encounter do not, nor should they, replace the cultural assets that you bring with you to the postsecondary campus. Rather, think of them as expanding your ability to move in and out of a greater number of social settings with grace, humanity, and success. That is, you are making the world in which you walk bigger!

It is also simply a fact that there is no way for you to put your cultural identities aside. You cannot, in any honest way, leave your sociocultural (racial and ethnic) identities behind you when you step onto a college campus and a classroom. Rather we encourage you to enter these spaces embracing your full, authentic, cultural self.

These are just a few reasons why we wish you to regard your cultural and ancestral knowledges as assets.

We know that, as an ISOC, and especially if you are the first in your family to go to college, you are not always aware of the specific and unique opportunities available to you to develop and strengthen your cultural and linguistic assets—a topic we turn to next.

ANCESTRAL CAPITAL

Ancestral capital refers to the "ways of knowing" from your ancestors (beliefs, stories, narratives, images, recordings, texts, etc.). It includes your understanding of ancestral ways of knowing, and how these ways of knowing can be used to guide you in connecting and grounding you in your origins and identity, your place in the world, your relationships with others, and how you meet all the challenges you may face in life including how to succeed in postsecondary education.

Knowing the difficulties your ancestors went through, whether 50 or 500 years ago, can help inspire you to follow their examples toward success.

A key component of ancestral capital is knowing that you are setting an example—and creating a narrative—for the generations who will come after you. At the very least, ancestral capital can ground you in the beliefs and values passed down to you that guide you in all your endeavors. In short, ancestral capital can provide you with a sense of *not-aloneness* in all your endeavors.

IDENTIFYING YOUR CULTURAL ASSETS

Identifying your cultural assets is not easy; recall that culture is often invisible to us and part of our "collective unconscious" (Jung, 1981).

One way to begin to identify your cultural assets is to think of things such as objects or products that represent your cultural identity. These might include objects such as family heirlooms, clothes that represent who you are culturally, or games you love playing with your friends and family.

At another level, think about practices that feel comfortable to you. These might be learning by observing more than listening, making sure your elders have been served before you feel comfortable serving yourself, gift giving when meeting long-lost relatives and other practices.

At yet another level, think of values that are central to your cultural identity. These might include, for example, the importance of family, the value of building relationships, the respect for elders, and the importance of generosity.

Finally, at the deepest (but harder to identify) level are those things that shape your worldview. Examples might be seeing things in nature as living beings, a belief in many gods, and a reverence more for the past than for the future.

> ***Think Alone/Think Together:*** Given this description of cultural capital, make an initial list of some of your most important cultural assets. What is included? What is not a central part, given the description, of your cultural identity? Which parts of culture do you still wonder about?

YOUR CULTURAL CAPITAL: PITFALLS AND CAVEATS

While we see cultural assets as beneficial to you as you move into postsecondary education, not everyone that you will interact with will see them as positives. We deeply know that it is hard to learn from someone who puts down or dismisses your race or ethnicity. No one wants to learn in a setting where they feel like who they are is unimportant or where a part of their identity is being belittled.

When you feel like your identity and your integrity are being questioned and devalued, you may not want to put your full self into what you are learning, understandably. You may find yourself resisting this negativity to your identity by refusing to learn from that person or from those materials. This is a reaction known as "willful not learning" (Kohl, 1994) and is often a reasonable reaction given how difficult it can be to go on learning as if nothing happened.

With respect to cultural assets, some people hold and communicate racist views of Indigenous People and People of Color generally and may even target their prejudicial comments to you directly. While we wish and hope that this will not be the case, we want you to be prepared for such negativity before it occurs. We do so knowing that you have, most likely, already experienced bias, prejudice, and discrimination—in either explicit/overt forms or via implicit/veiled forms.

Whole books have been written about these forms of ignorance, negativity, and hatred. What we provide is a thumbnail sketch of racism (as just one of many kinds of oppression), the forms it can take, and initial ways of responding when you have these encounters.

UNDERSTANDING THE FOUNDATIONS OF RACISM

We begin by defining some key terms. **Stereotypes** are those "reduced or simplified characteristics attributed to a group" (Sensoy & DiAngelo, 2017, p. 52) of people based on their identities, such as race, ethnicity, language, religion, sexual identity, and sexual orientation. **Prejudice** comes into play when we assign a value to our stereotypes. More specifically, prejudice is defined as "learned prejudgments ... and refers to internal thoughts, feelings, attitudes, and assumptions" (Sensoy & DiAngelo, p. 51) about people from different social groups based upon stereotypes. **Discrimination** takes this one step further. Discrimination occurs when people act on their prejudices. These actions may be overt and explicit such as threats, slander, and ridicule. Or they can be covert and implicit such as someone who is prejudiced against Vietnamese people and therefore ignores or avoids Vietnamese students they encounter.

> ***Think Alone/Think Together:*** Think about an instance where you know you were experiencing racism or where you wondered if racism was at play? What happened? What did you think? How did you feel? How did you respond?

Racism, in the U.S. context, is defined by Sensoy and DiAngelo (2017) as the "cultural prejudice and discrimination, supported intentionally or unintentionally by institutional power and authority, used to the advantage of Whites and the disadvantage of peoples of color" (p. 124). That is, it is a marriage of both ideas (prejudice) and actions (discrimination) that leads to racial inequities (Kendi, 2019).

Cultural (and Ancestral) Capital

It is those with power and authority, historically and contemporarily, who support and advance racism in both policy and practice, whether they do so purposefully (intentionally) or inadvertently (unintentionally). Stated more directly, racism is a product of both prejudice and power (prejudice + power = racism). Racism exists at both interpersonal levels (evident in person-to-person interactions) and in institutions (evident in policies and practices).

The Four "I's" of Oppression

Racism is one form of oppression. **Oppression** is the "systematic abuse, exploitation and injustice" (Cuauhtin, 2019b, p. 217) by dominant groups against those who are subordinate. Racism, as with many other forms of oppression, shows up in many ways. An informative and useful framework to consider is the four "I's" of oppression (Bell, 2013): ideological, institutional, interpersonal, and internalized (see Cuauhtin, 2019b, pp. 216–219 for an extended discussion of these).

Ideological oppression is the idea that one group of people, based on any number of demographic differences, is better than another and therefore has a right to dominate the other group. It often shows up in the descriptor words used by the dominant group (better, stronger, smarter, etc.) when describing the subordinate group (less than, weaker, dumber, etc.)

Institutional oppression is the idea that, based on ideological oppression, the control of one group over another is justified. This control occurs in the policies, procedures, and practices of major institutions such as the legal system, the banking system, the political system, and the education system, to name just a few. That is, those in control structure these institutions—and their policies, procedures, and practices—in ways that maintain and strengthen the dominant group at the expense of (and sometimes on the backs of) the subordinated group. Of note, when this occurs, whether intentional or not, it is still institutional oppression.

Interpersonal oppression is the idea that one person or group of people has the right to dehumanize, in many ways, another person or another group of people. They do so because they believe themselves superior (ideological oppression). Additionally, they sense that the institutions (schools, police, media, etc.) will support, or at least ignore, their behavior (institutional oppression). When most people discuss forms of oppression, it is often focused at the level of interpersonal oppression.

Internalized oppression is the idea that some members of subordinated groups will come to believe the negative ideas about them and their group (ideological oppression). It is reinforced by their lack of access and decision-making in schools, courts, banks (institutional oppression). It is re-emphasized when they have day-to-day encounters of disrespect and dehumanization (interpersonal oppression). Internalized oppression is no accident; rather, it is purposeful. Brazilian educator and philosopher Paolo Freire claims that "the role of the dominant ideology is to inculcate in the oppressed a sense of blame and culpability about their situation of oppression" (Freire, 2000, p. 58).

Once internalized oppression occurs, individuals begin to oppress themselves (e.g., not apply for a scholarship, back down from asking for a deserved promotion, etc.) and sometimes even oppress members of their own communities. They often do so as a result of feeling angry, powerless, and frustrated. Lashing out at others in subordinated groups is one highly negative way of feeling like one is in control.

A few notes here about internalized oppression. First, internalized oppression is the result of outside forces (ideological, institutional, and interpersonal forms of oppression). It is not the fault of an individual from a subordinated social-identity group. Second, even though individuals may feel these forces of oppression, it does not mean that their life must be dictated by these. Third, once you can see and name these forms of oppression, you can push against them. You can do so by questioning statements/assumptions about one group's superiority over another, by calling out forms of discrimination when evident in our institutions, and by challenging those who discriminate against you, your group, or those from other subordinated groups.

> ***Think Alone/Think Together:*** What is your reaction to the four "I's" of oppression? What makes sense? What is unclear? How would you describe this to someone who feels like they just experienced discrimination?

Cultural (and Ancestral) Capital

In pushing against the various forms of oppression, we encourage you to consider the following:

- Look for those from your racial or ethnic community who are anti-oppressive leaders to support them while observing how they engage in this important work.
- Develop a network of individuals committed to racial and social justice.
- Learn about the histories, contributions, and assets of your particular social-identity group.
- Ally with other social-identity groups to help build a stronger social justice movement.

An Extended Example

The four forms of oppression identified here are linked and overlap with each other while also mutually reinforcing each other. You can think of them as four interrelated circles of oppression (Figure 4.2). Because this is such an important topic, but also that takes time to fully grasp, we provide an extended example here that we hope might promote their greater understanding. We use the example of why some ISOC are not as successful in school (recall these gaps identified in the prologue) as other groups of students.

On the ideological level, some people believe that students from certain sociocultural identity backgrounds are genetically deficient and inferior. Others assert that the lack of a traditional family structure, the two-parent family, is the problem. Yet others argue that there is something in the group's cultural values themselves (being more relationship-oriented than task-oriented, for example) that works against educational success. Still another group would argue that poor life choices are the problem. These and other deficit-oriented ideologies like them are used to explain differences in academic achievement.

On the institutional level, schools employ a variety of practices associated with these ideologies. The most important is that the school blames the students, their families, and their communities for the problems students encounter in school. Given this, there is no need to change what is being taught, how it is being taught, or how it is being assessed. At the same time,

Figure 4.2. Circles of Oppression

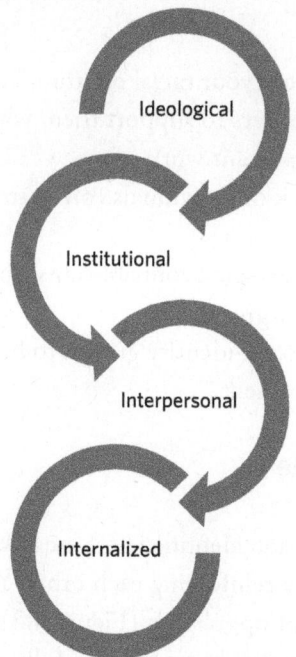

the school may actively work to change the students' cultural values by way of **assimilation**. The decision to focus the curriculum on a Eurocentric view of the world is but one (of many other) active oppressive institutional practices based on deficit ideologies.

At the interpersonal level, you may hear teachers and others state that parents of ISOC just do not care about education. They may express directly that the parents are the problem or that the cultural values of the student are holding them back from pursuing a postsecondary degree. They may bemoan the fact, in staff meetings, that Parents of Color did not come to the teacher–parent conferences as proof. They do so without bothering to consider other reasons why these parents may not have shown up for those meetings such as work conflicts, childcare issues, transportation challenges, etc.

At the internalized level, the students will come to believe that they are, indeed, not smart, or capable, or "college-material." Given this, they may give up even trying to learn; after all, the students may think, what is the point if they just are not smart enough. They may not see much reason in even attending school and, instead, feel that their potential is unseen or not valued.

We hope that by providing this extended example you can see why the four I's of oppression framework is so important for understanding the various ways oppression plays out. We also hope you can see why a capital- and assets-based framework can be so powerful and transformative. A capital- and assets-based approach calls on us to think critically about taken-for-granted norms and assumptions and challenges us to identify underlying ideologies, to name oppressive institutional policies and practices, and to push against our interactions with others who explain deficiencies as the root problem. A capital and assets mindset helps us reject oppressive ideologies and gives us tools to work against them.

In sum, we hope you have a stronger sense of how racism plays out as understood from the lens of the four dominant forms of oppression. You may be able to look back at some of your own experiences and now be able to name what was occurring. While we certainly hope you will not experience these once you are on a postsecondary campus, we urge you to prepare yourself for these various forms of oppression when and if they occur. We urge you to rise above and beyond these. To that end, we will discuss the kinds of pitfalls you may experience and how to effectively deal with them in greater detail in Chapter 9, the Humanization Capital chapter.

STRENGTHENING YOUR CULTURAL AND ANCESTRAL ASSETS

It is often the case that ISOC arrive on campus with a strong sense of racial and/or ethnic identity. This is especially true if you have grown up in a family and community that encourages and values the heritages present in that community. We believe you will benefit by deepening what you can learn about your heritage that might go beyond what you may have learned in school and even, to some degree, what you have learned in your heritage family and community.

However, it is also true that some ISOC arriving at a college campus have been raised in a dominant European-American cultural setting or where other races and ethnicities were not valued. That is, you—and others of a shared ancestral background—may be going into higher education with a slight but emerging understanding of your racial and/or ethnic identity. Do not think of this unexplored but emerging ability to understand your cultural background as your fault. Recognize that for a long time public schooling in the United States has focused on getting students and their families to conform to the dominant mainstream culture. This process is called cultural assimilation.

Wherever you land on this continuum—from fully aware of your culture and cultural identity or emerging in the understanding of your heritage culture—most higher education settings provide opportunities to renew and strengthen your cultural assets.

> ***Think Alone/Think Together:*** Where do you stand on the continuum between being fully aware of your cultural identity and being somewhere in the process of coming to greater awareness? What do you need most to help you to come to greater awareness?

The opportunities to renew and strengthen your cultural assets can be found in many places within your postsecondary institution.

Opportunities via Academic Majors

At one level, in almost every field of study, you will find individuals whose academic research focuses on ethnic and/or racial diversity. This is especially true in the social sciences (history, political science, sociology, etc.). But even in some Science, Technology, Engineering, and Math (STEM) programs, people are exploring reasons why many ISOC are not choosing their fields and how to more appropriately welcome them in, or they are incorporating "Indigenous Ways of Knowing" into classes or are identifying important individuals from diverse backgrounds who made significant contributions to their fields. Accordingly, no matter which academic major you might choose, there are likely opportunities for you to expand and deepen your knowledge of your cultural identity.

Opportunities via Ethnic/Cultural Studies

Courses in ethnic/cultural studies—sometimes connected with women and gender studies—provide opportunities to learn about the histories, contemporary challenges, approaches to resisting oppression, and hopes and dreams of their respective communities. Sometimes these courses have a general focus on many ethnic/racial groups (such as ethnic studies). And sometimes these courses are race- (Black or African American studies) or ethnic-specific (Chicano studies).

We think ethnic/cultural studies programs and courses are some of the best places to not only learn (or learn more deeply) about your own and other ethnic groups while, at the same time, finding others who share a similar interest. Because we think so much of ethnic/cultural studies as a place to find yourself, we will share more about these programs in later chapters.

Opportunities via Class Assignments

At the same time, there are often opportunities to explore, deepen, and affirm your cultural assets even outside of ethnic/cultural studies, programs, and courses. Teachers often create assignments designed to allow you to include your own self-interests. For example, a course in history may allow you to write a paper or give a presentation on some historical moment of your own choosing. You can use that assignment to explore a historical moment related to your racial or ethnic group's experience.

One thing we are sure you will come to learn is that there is a wide range of ways of being from a

> **PRO TIP:** Consider taking classes in the various ethnic studies programs that may be available on the campus where you find yourself. Start with those classes most closely linked to your own cultural and linguistic heritage. They often spur greater pride and deepen your understanding of sociocultural identities. It also helps you to value and appreciate, as well as explore and honor, the many, many ways of being a member of the groups with which you identify.

> **PRO TIP:** If asked to share your experience as a member of a racial and/or ethnic social identity group, take care to "personalize" your response by saying "My experience has been" or "There are many ways to be from my community, so I can't speak for everyone, but here's how I understand it." In this way, you are clear that you are not speaking for an entire group of people.

particular ethnic, cultural, racial, or social-identity group. That is, there is more than one way to be Indigenous, or Black or Latine, for example. That is the beauty of the opportunity to explore culture and language via class assignments.

We are mindful, ourselves, that even while we are from ethnic/racial communities, we cannot speak for all ethnic groups nor for all the people in a specific community even when we belong to that community. Because of that, we want to be careful to point out that you should not be seen as the one spokesperson for your entire community. One person does not represent their whole community.

We want to be clear that while we think you can use your cultural assets as you are educating yourself, as well as to educate others, we urge you to do so because you want to and not because you feel obliged to share these assets with others.

Opportunities via Connecting With Indigenous Faculty/Staff and Faculty/Staff of Color

While it is true that the number of Indigenous Faculty and Faculty of Color in higher education is low, it is likely you will encounter some in the courses you take and programs you pursue. Reaching out to Indigenous Faculty/Staff and Faculty/Staff of Color is a good way to minimize any feelings of isolation you may be experiencing. While also serving as role models of success for you, they often are a good source of specific information about how to navigate your postsecondary education institution and the specific opportunities available to ISOC. Recognize that many Indigenous Faculty and Faculty of Color were motivated to be successful because they want to be able to support the next generation of young people from their heritage community. You assist them when you seek them out and ask their advice.

At another level, your presence in their classes and offices might also be helpful to these Indigenous Faculty and Faculty of Color who may be experiencing isolation.

At the same time, we certainly hope you will find great allies in White faculty and staff. Depending upon where you attend postsecondary education, you may end up in a college or university where the number of Indigenous Faculty/Staff and Faculty/Staff of Color is extremely limited. Looking for those White allies among the faculty and staff will be extremely helpful for you.

Opportunities via Student Social-Identity Clubs

Beyond programs, courses, assignments, and Faculty of Color, you can enhance, strengthen, and affirm your cultural assets beyond the academic curriculum through **extracurriculars**—those activities pursued beyond the normal courses and activities assigned in classrooms. For example, the postsecondary education campus where you may attend, especially if there are low numbers of ISOC, could have "multicultural" clubs that bring groups from multiple racial and ethnic backgrounds together to support each other. On campuses with greater numbers of ISOC, you may encounter ethnic or race-specific student clubs. This might include student collectives such as Native American Student Union, Pacific Islander Student Association, Movimiento Estudiantil Chicanos de Aztlán (Chicano/Mexican-American), Black Student Alliance (Black) or other similarly named organizations.

Beyond finding a group of potential friends and a support network you can access, these student-led clubs often provide opportunities to develop and strengthen your leadership skills. Some offer cultural programming not only for their members but for those from the broader campus and local community as well. Additionally, they often serve as an important voice to those on the campus about ways to make the campus more inclusive and affirming for current and future generations of ISOC.

Opportunities via Student Support Services

All college campuses have some kind of student support services whose mission is to support student success. While some of these student services support all students on campus, it is often the case that there are support services explicitly seeking the academic and social success of ISOC.

Sometimes these are located within the general student support services offices. At other times, campuses have created their own space, programs, and staff dedicated just to supporting and affirming ISOC. It may also be true, typically on those college campuses where there are large numbers of ISOC, that there is a student support service office specific to one social-identity group such as a "longhouse" for Indigenous students.

We strongly urge you to learn about these offices, meet the people who work there, and understand the support services they can provide before a problem or challenge arises. These individuals and offices—whose job it is to help you be successful—can be some of the best advocates you can find on campus.

A couple of notes about what we have shared thus far regarding strengthening your cultural assets. While we have focused on opportunities via ethnic and racial courses, coursework, faculty, student clubs and student support services, recognize that there are often great opportunities that are not directly connected to your cultural heritage. You might find faculty advocates from a range of backgrounds. A student chess club or *intramural sports* (recreational sports organized inside the institution for fun, friendship, and fitness) might be a source of fulfillment for you. The counseling office, as part of student support services, might be just what you need to help you through a crisis or to minimize anxiety you might be experiencing such as the stress of standardized exams.

A second note is to think about those opportunities that go beyond the boundaries of the college or university. Sometimes you can find cultural affirmation in the local community where the campus is located. Seek out those local community-based organizations. Go to those cultural events hosted by the community. Find those places where people from your racial/ethnic group congregate (such as grocery stores, churches/temples, etc.). These are just a few ways to maintain and strengthen your cultural assets.

Cultural (and Ancestral) Capital

A third note is to find ways, based on your cultural and linguistic assets, to contribute to those who will follow in your footsteps. You might volunteer as a tutor to another ISOC, or work with a local cultural community organization, or return to your high school to share your experiences in postsecondary education. While we absolutely encourage you to use the resources on campus to help you thrive, we also encourage you to recognize the incredible resources and assets you bring that can inspire those who may walk in your footsteps.

We hope you have found this chapter helpful for understanding a central part of your response to the question you probably often ask yourself: Who Am I? There are parts of your identity that are personal and parts of your identity that are social. We urge you to understand and grow in your sociocultural identity.

Fully grasping the four "I's" of oppression will help you respond to those instances where you experience personally, or see others experience, oppression. Understanding how oppression often operates on four levels should help you make sense of those instances.

All of this is part of our encouragement for you to bring your full authentic self to postsecondary education. Not only will you feel better about yourself, but it will foster more authentic relationships with others that you may meet. We also believe that being centered in your sociocultural identity will serve you well in successfully completing your academic coursework. In short, just be you, fully and authentically.

Finally, recognize that we are all, in various ways, coming to greater awareness of our sociocultural identities. While we may bring much of this from our home communities, we hope you find comfort in knowing that there will be opportunities in postsecondary education, as in all you do over your lifetime, for continual growth and exploration aimed at becoming who you are, fully and authentically.

In this, consider the guidance from Thích Nhất Hạnh (2007), Vietnamese philosopher and peace activist, when he wrote: "To be beautiful means to be yourself... If you crave acceptance and recognition and try to change yourself to fit what other people want you to be, you will suffer all your life. True happiness and true power lie in understanding yourself, accepting yourself, having confidence in yourself" (p. 103).

END OF CHAPTER ACTIVITY: FINDING YOUR CULTURAL ASSETS

To help you identify and understand your cultural assets, we invite you to engage in the following activities:

1. Answer the question "Who Am I?" socially and culturally by identifying 3–5 of the most important parts of your sociocultural identity. Then identify whether these identities are valued (dominant) in the mainstream or not valued (nondominant). What do these parts of your identity mean to you?
2. Tell a story about something you experienced that represents or really speaks to who you are culturally (racially or ethnically or both).
3. Share a piece of art (music, artwork, poem, rap, movie, etc.) that you identify with and that speaks to your identity. Consider the following:
    a. Identify a piece of art or a movie or a song that you feel powerfully represents your culture.
    b. Reflect upon why you chose that particular creative piece.
    c. How does that creative piece highlight the strengths of your family, culture, and identity?
    d. What specific parts of that creative piece would you want to share with others you might meet and want to connect with on your journey in postsecondary education—your roommates in a dorm, your professors, etc.
    e. Prompted by the creative piece, what stories might you tell and share about your own life?
4. Do an Internet search for "Who I Am" poems. After looking at instructions and examples, write your own Who I Am poem.
5. Write a racial autobiography by using the following writing prompts: https://www.pps.net/cms/lib/OR01913224

/Centricity/Domain/3992//Equity/Racial%20Autobiography%20Questions.pdf

6. For those of you who want to go deeper into the many facets of your sociocultural identity, do an outline of a critical family history. Consider Sleeter's (2023) description of critical family history to help you think about that history. Note that there are several engaging examples in the journal Genealogy (2020, Vol. 4, No. 2) where individuals detail their critical family history as part of a larger autoethnobiography.

FIVE

Linguistic Capital
Valuing Your Language(s)

Around the middle of the summer, the professor starts class with a small-group activity. She poses the following prompt for the small groups: (1) discuss their own experiences around learning and speaking languages other than English; and (2) raise at least one question each group has about language diversity.

Three of the five friends (Josephine, Teew, and Pancho), sitting next to each other, join up with another student named Virginia who happens to sit close by. Anna and Kieran, sitting a little farther away, end up in another small group.

Josephine starts by saying that as an African American she is uncertain how to reply. She acknowledges that some members of her extended family speak "Black English," which is typical of some Black communities, especially in more urban areas. She asks: Is Black English even a language?

Teew says that he speaks some of his native language and is taking classes at a local cultural community center aimed at "language revitalization." He mentions that speaking a native language was banned in boarding schools and other public places for many decades, and now there are so few native speakers of the language still living. Teew wants to know more about language revitalization.

Virginia, a White student, says her home language is English. She took Spanish classes in high school to connect with an increasing number of Spanish-speaking newcomers. She says she doesn't feel like her Spanish skills go beyond offering simple greetings. She says learning a different language is hard. She asks: What can we do if we want to learn a new language?

Pancho mentions that, given Josephine's comment, he speaks Chicano English. Up to that point, he hadn't considered it as a language. While his family speaks both English and Spanish at home, he says that he speaks Spanish but is not really sure if he can say he speaks it fully. He struggled in his advanced Spanish language class in high school when they were reading the Spanish novelist Cervantes's *Don Quixote*. Pancho's question is: Why was this advanced Spanish language course so hard, given his ability to communicate in Spanish with everyone in his family?

INTRODUCTION TO LINGUISTIC CAPITAL

In Chapter 4 we explored the importance of our cultural and ancestral capital. In a way, we could have combined that chapter with this one as language and culture are so intertwined. That is, language reflects culture and culture is learned through language. It is also true that language sometimes even shapes culture.

As with culture, our language abilities—and sometimes the lack thereof in terms of speaking ancestral languages—are often a significant part of our overall sociocultural identities. Language is a central part of what it means when we identify ourselves as a "Native Tsalagi-speaker" (language of the Cherokee Nation) or a "learner of Cebuano" (language of the Philippines province of Cebu) or an "English-dominant Latino."

Language also ties people together. Hearing someone speak a language familiar to you, especially when it is not the nation's dominant language, opens a door to a relationship and strengthens ties. Finding ways to communicate in other languages, dialects, and styles helps to build bridges across other kinds of differences (e.g., race, gender, economic class, etc.). It is through language that our families grow together and our communities move toward unity.

> **PRO TIP:** Remember that language and culture are deeply connected. Understanding how they are connected helps you to appreciate and value your own cultural and linguistic assets while affirming the greater diversity of our world.

> ***Think Alone/Think Together:*** What do you already know about your family's experience with speaking languages other than English? What about their experiences learning to speak English?

At the same time, language use can sometimes feel like it is being used to exclude. Exclusion might happen, for example, when parents speak a native language but their children do not. The native language serves as private communication meant just for them. It might also be used in a school setting where students use a common non-English language to go deeper on a class project or to share some of the latest gossip.

Because language is such a big part of culture, efforts aimed at cultural assimilation have often included prohibiting—sometimes even punishing—the speaking of Indigenous languages in an effort to eradicate these ancestral languages altogether. One goal of cultural assimilation has included *linguicide*, or the death of a language. The result is that some Indigenous languages are now extinct, while a substantial number are on the verge of extinction (Goodman, 2023), with few people speaking them, and many of those speakers being elderly.

Beyond prohibiting the speaking of Indigenous languages, eradicating an Indigenous language stops the teaching among community members of Native ways of thinking and knowing. It distances students from family members, relatives, and elders. And, as a means of control of an oppressed group, it strengthens efforts at cultural assimilation.

The United States has a long history of promoting linguistic assimilation. While there were eras in our history when language diversity was promoted—such as during wartime when we needed people to translate—the majority of U.S. history is characterized by efforts to minimize linguistic diversity. It has included efforts to prevent speaking languages other than English in schools, in banks, and in the court system.

In this chapter, we explore linguistic capital. To do so, we identify a few key ideas about the nature of language. We describe why language is an asset. From there, we will help you identify your linguistic asset. We will describe instances of oppression around language by defining and discussing linguicism. We end with suggestions around strengthening your linguistic assets.

> ***Think Alone/Think Together:*** Given the questions posed by the professor in the opening vignette for this chapter, how would you describe your own language experiences and abilities? What questions do you have about linguistic capital?

EXPLORING LINGUISTIC CAPITAL

In the Introduction of this book, we defined *linguistic capital* as "the intellectual and social skills learned through communication experiences in more than one language and/or style" (Cuauhtin, 2019a, p. 248). It might include one's knowledge and use of cultural metaphors, Indigenous languages, and regional language variations (such as Tex-Mex; Nevárez, 2022).

Language is not just a conglomeration of words and sentences we use. It is through speaking with others who share our language heritage that we develop new insights, hear other worldviews, clarify our own viewpoints, and share our joys, hopes, passions, and sorrows. As mentioned, it is through language that we develop and nurture relationships.

As you may have noticed from previous definitions and descriptors in Chapter 4, language is a big part of culture. At one level, it is clearly a part of the surface level of culture, since hearing or seeing someone speak a language that is not the dominant language of a society is easily observable. Hearing someone speaking Urdu, or Spanish, or Tlingit might serve for you as an example of language diversity.

Consider some other simple differences across languages that you may readily notice even if you speak just a little of the other language.

Languages differ in the labels used for things (such as "jabon" in Spanish for "soap" in English). This is called a *semantic difference*. Be aware that many single words may have multiple meanings. The word "chair" in English could mean the thing you sit on, or the title and role you hold such as chair of the

Register to Vote Committee at your school. Consider how words change or expand meaning over time, such as the word "mouse."

You may note that there are differences in grammar, which are called *syntactic differences*. As but one simple and commonly known example, in Spanish the descriptor word or adjective comes after the noun (person, place or thing). Thus, in Spanish, "White House" is "Casa Blanca" (House White) in Spanish. In Mandarin, a speaker may say, "I went to 3 restaurant" since the number "3" is all that is needed to mark the plural.

Another difference among languages, though perhaps a bit harder to notice, is in how and when language can be used, which is called *pragmatics*. For example, when passing someone on the street, you may say "How are you?" If the person stops and proceeds to share, in extended detail, how they are doing physically, mentally, and emotionally, you might be stunned into silence. That is because we all interact within specific social, cultural, and linguistic expectations or norms (i.e., pragmatics) when we use language. Pragmatically, you meant "How are you?" to be a variation of "hello," to which the person addressed should reply a short "I'm fine" or "I'm doing well" or "I'm okay." Pragmatically, you expected a short list of short potential replies. However, a speaker familiar with a different language's pragmatics may believe you want to hear a long explanation about how they are doing.

As an additional example, think about all the unwritten rules you might be following when taking a computer into a repair shop and interacting with the technician. These might include, for instance, who speaks first, who asks questions, how you answer questions, how much you share about yourself, what information they will want to collect from you, how you will know what you can expect from them.

While there are surface and just-below-the-surface differences in languages, there are also deep (and often hidden) differences. That is because language often conveys certain norms or values. Consider how in Spanish (among other languages) there are different ways of addressing a person based on how familiar or formal you are with them. Spanish-speakers will use the word "tú" with a friend or another student but will use the word "usted" when speaking to an elder or a professor. English-speakers, by contrast, would just use the word "you" whether we are speaking to a friend or a professor.

This difference mirrors the greater awareness Spanish speakers have, in this example, of different levels (*statuses*) of relationships people might have

Linguistic Capital

with each other. In this example, the language use difference, for Spanish-speakers, tells them that how we view others in relation to ourselves is important.

> ***Think Alone/Think Together:*** What have been some of your own examples of understanding the differences between languages you know and how other languages are used? Share an instance where you were misunderstood (or you misunderstood others) as a result of language differences.

To be sure, our linguistic assets go beyond the ability to speak a particular language. They also refer to a person's "ability to work within different language registers and communication styles" (Office of Faculty Development, n.d., para 1) as well as dialects that help them to understand and be understood in a variety of settings.

A *language register* describes the different ways we speak given whom we are speaking to and where the language is being spoken (Diaz-Rico, 2017). For example, consider how a parent speaks to their infant children (this is called "motherese") differently than when speaking to an adult. As another example, notice how people change the way they speak when they think someone is not a native English speaker.

Communication style difference refers to the various ways you might want to speak that range from passive to assertive. For example, rather than answering a request directly by saying "No, I will not do this," your communication style may be more passive, and you might say, "That would be very difficult."

The Oxford English Dictionary (n.d.) defines *dialect* as a "particular form of language peculiar to a specific region or social group." It includes the unique ways words are pronounced (*accents*), distinctive words and phrases, and even different grammar structures. Speaking a dialect may signal where a person comes from (for example, the southern part of the United States or the East Coast) as well as build solidarity among speakers of a particular dialect. It also expands where and with whom communication can occur.

> ***Think Alone/Think Together:*** Take note of the registers, communication styles, and dialects that you find yourself using in different situations. Name these. How do these help you to develop relationships with others?

A few key ideas are important at this point. First, we encourage you to not make a value judgment based on language differences. It is incorrect to assume that one form of language, communication style, dialect, or accent is better than others. These are just differences and show the beauty of our ability to communicate.

Second, expanding your linguistic assets in terms of learning new languages, registers, communication styles, and dialects will serve you well as you move into a variety of social settings where the ability to use a variety of language assets will be important. The ability to communicate effectively expands who can be part of your world. We will come back to this idea later in this chapter.

Third, we surmise that you may already speak more than one language, adapt your register depending upon who you are communicating with, and change your communication style as appropriate. You already speak a dialect and may speak with an accent. Thus, you already have demonstrated your *ability to expand* your linguistic assets, given past experiences. This will assist you well in postsecondary education, where a big part of being successful academically entails your ability to learn the linguistic tools to communicate within a particular academic field of study.

Before going on, we want you to understand that you may hear someone asking you or someone else to speak in "standard" English. This assumes that there is only one right or wrong way to speak a language. Within English, for example, whose language is standard? Is it the English spoken in the United States, Australia, England, or Canada?

There are lots of variations of every language. As a result, identifying what is "standard" is often a problem. Add to this that every language also has a variety of accents and dialects. These all are central to the beauty of all languages.

> **PRO TIP:** Regard Black English (and all language varieties) as a complex language that can communicate the world of ideas as well as other languages. In doing so, you are affirming the many ways in which people speak to each other and, most importantly, connect on a familiar basis.

One prominent example is Ebonics. *Ebonics*, also known as African American Vernacular English or Black English, is a word that combines "Black" and "Phonics." Some have come to regard Black English as an inferior dialect of English. More recently, Ebonics has been identified as a legitimate language, not a dialect, with its own distinct vocabulary, grammar structure, and forms of use.

YOUR LINGUISTIC ASSETS

You likely already speak a dialect of, or language beyond, English. We encourage you to continue to strengthen and use your linguistic assets to help you as a learner. We do so because knowing more than one language has many benefits (Skibba, 2018). Bilingual individuals think more flexibly and creatively. They also tend to be more open-minded. Because language conveys a way of thinking, speaking more than one language, or using more than one communication style, fosters a different way of thinking and talking about the world.

Recall from Chapter 4 that learning, whether at home or at school, happens in interaction with others; that is, learning is a social activity. Language and dialects are a big part of those interactions. Formal schooling, in particular, happens via particular ways of communicating, which requires learners to understand the language and communication styles spoken in school-based settings. Given your linguistic assets, and the fact that you were successful in school, you have already demonstrated that you can learn the language and dialects that are important in school-based settings.

With respect to language, you likely have developed a toolbox of different languages, registers, communication styles, and dialects to be successful outside and inside of schools. You have been developing your academic language of different disciplines when you took history, science, math, art, and music classes. In other words, you have learned how to learn about the languages used in different academic disciplines. Be prepared to realize that much of what you learn in a postsecondary setting is centered on deepening your language skills, including new words often associated with new ideas, and new ways of talking about the academic topics you will encounter.

> **PRO TIP:** Consider taking classes in linguistics if you find yourself interested in knowing more about the complexity of languages. Linguistics classes help you to understand how languages, all kinds of languages, are structured, used, and operate in ways that help its members to accomplish important activities.

Beyond helping you within your own family and community, speaking languages and dialects different from the mainstream allows you to successfully walk within different kinds of sociocultural and linguistic settings—such as local communities, schools, and organizations—that make up our diverse democracy. It should not come as a surprise that employers are looking for employees who speak more than one language.

These are just a few reasons why we wish you to regard your linguistic assets as important. Taking stock of these assets is a topic we discuss next.

IDENTIFYING YOUR LINGUISTIC ASSETS

Identifying your linguistic assets is, in many ways, much easier than identifying your cultural assets.

Consider the different languages that you have learned to speak. Also, consider how you change your registers and communication styles when using a language depending on whom you are speaking to and for what purpose.

One special consideration to ponder is how well you can speak a language. For example, are you proficient enough to read an academic paper or attend a lecture in that language? One important distinction to be aware of

> **PRO TIP:** Be aware of the difference between interpersonal language skills used with friends and family and academic language skills, the kinds required when taking classes in that language. Knowing this difference will help you to understand both the level of your own language abilities but also assure you are not making faulty assumptions about someone else's abilities.

around your language assets is the difference between *interpersonal language* (the language spoken to a friend or used to get directions, for example) versus *academic language* (the kind spoken in schools and in postsecondary institutions).

Another consideration is around the dialects that you speak with family, friends, and neighbors. To better identify dialects, consider how you change your communication and speech when you are at home with your parents and grandparents versus when you are out and about with friends in the neighborhood where you grew up. Consider whether or not you use those same dialects outside of your community or when you are not in your friendship network.

Considering both language and dialects you use will help give you a sense of your linguistic assets.

As with all the assets we describe in this book, we highly encourage you to develop, strengthen, and maximize your linguistic assets. Consider your linguistic skills and flexibility as a major asset that sets you apart from others, increases your social networks, and expands your understanding of the world.

YOUR LINGUISTIC CAPITAL: PITFALLS AND CAVEATS

Unfortunately, we also know that some settings as well as people you interact with may be unwelcoming toward individuals who speak different languages and dialects. **Linguicism** is often at play in these examples. Linguicism is the "ideologies, structures and practices" that create unequal differences in power and access to resources based on language (Skutnabb-Kangas, 2015, p. 1). At its heart, linguicism is a form of oppression associated with the belief that some languages and dialects are better than others and therefore more deserving of status, honor, and acceptance.

We encourage you to use the oppression framework—the four "I's" of oppression that we described in detail in Chapter 4—to understand how linguicism plays out and how speaking languages other than English can often be negatively received.

We are deliberately returning to the four "I's" of oppression framework for three reasons. First, we think it is a helpful framework to describe how linguicism plays out. Second, it can be a difficult framework to grasp fully so we hope these additional extended examples might be helpful. Finally, we hope it solidifies how you can use this framework to make sense of things you may experience and, as important, to name them as an oppressive force at work.

Extended Example #1: Linguistic Oppression and Bilingual Education

The following example deals with bilingualism and bilingual education.

On an ideological level, some believe that English is a superior language to all other languages and that a "standard" dialect of English is also more valuable than others. This is a dangerous belief, on one hand, and conflicts with the understanding that all languages are complex and have the capacity to explain the world of thoughts, emotions, objects, and more. Nonetheless, many do carry this ideological belief and it shapes how they think and act.

On the institutional level, most of our systems (banking, schooling, the law, media, etc.) operate in ways that place English first and use English as the dominant language, sometimes almost exclusively. These systems could operate in any (or any combination of) language. Bilingual education is relatively rare, for example, even in schools where other languages besides English dominate and despite evidence of the power and importance of bilingualism (as described earlier in this chapter). On a broader level, there have even been attempts to make English the official language of the United States, such as with the policies advanced by an organization called "Official English" (also known informally as English-only). As you may know, the U.S. Constitution does not identify an official language for the country.

At the interpersonal level, individuals may ask others to stop speaking their native tongue, look on with disgust, or ask others to only speak English. For example, in 2017, a teacher in a New Jersey school district, where half of the students spoke Spanish at home, reprimanded three boys who were speaking Spanish and told them they needed to speak "American" (Benavides, 2017). We emphasize here the idea that this teacher was acting out a dominant ideology including the mistaken belief that language use signals one's national identity and allegiance. In this teacher's mind, the institution would support their reprimand of the students or at least not punish the teacher's action.

At the internalized level, it is true that some students may feel embarrassed to speak their native language in public places, especially when they have come to accept the belief that English is the only language of value. They may stop speaking the language at home, often at the expense of family relations, or may re-emphasize and redouble their efforts to speak English as fluently as possible, negating the development of their heritage language at the same time. Again, we point out that this is the result of the ideologies, the institutional policies and structures, and the ways that non-native speakers of English are treated by others.

Extended Example #2: Linguistic Oppression and Native Languages

Recall that we have discussed the importance of language as one part of one's cultural identity. It is through language that we come to know and embrace the worldview of the people who are most central in our lives in terms of family and community. It is through language that we develop the kinds of deep relationships with others from our social-identity groups, from our elders, our cousins, aunties and uncles and others.

It seems appropriate at this point to provide a brief sketch of efforts by Indigenous nations and their communities to revitalize their language. To do so, we first focus on just a few of the ways Indigenous peoples have experienced linguistic oppression.

Despite what we know about how important language is to any community, the United States set out to eradicate Indigenous languages and, in turn, the cultures from where they sprang. The goal of U.S. educational policy toward Indigenous people during the assimilationist period (1880s–1950s) was to kill them culturally in order to supposedly save them from what the United States perceived to be their inferior cultures. In a speech in 1892, Richard Pratt, the founder of the first Native American boarding school (the Carlisle Industrial School), stated, "All the Indian there is in the race should be dead. Kill the Indian in him, and save the man" (Pratt, 1892). U.S. educational policy sought to supposedly save the human being by eliminating who they were culturally and linguistically.

Fueling this push for eradication, at the ideological level, was a belief that the cultural identity and language capabilities of Indigenous people were inferior and should be erased.

At the institutional level, young people were sent off to boarding schools away from their home communities where their culture and language sprang. Their hair was cut, their clothes were burned, and they were given "American" names, among many other, more serious, forms of abuse they experienced. One significant practice, if not policy, was to ban speaking any language other than English.

This included, at the interpersonal level, actions such as the punishment of students who spoke their Native language by teachers and administrators. Classes were taught exclusively in English. Not only was the goal to diminish the Indigenous language of the individual in a school setting, but also to stop the communication link between them and the cultural knowledge of their home and nation.

As a result, largely because of these experiences in boarding schools, generations of Indigenous people unwillingly, at the internalized level, were forced to live out this ideology and became estranged from their ancestral languages.

Understanding how important language is to cultural revitalization, efforts are ongoing throughout Indigenous communities to recapture and revitalize these Indigenous languages. This includes promoting Indigenous languages in reservation schools, encouraging their use in public spaces, and advocating for their use in the business and political affairs of Indigenous nations.

These efforts are centered on expanding and uplifting the language and cultural wisdom held by the nations' elders. These elders are engaged in some

> **PRO TIP:** Be a strong advocate and ally for those working to engage in linguistic revitalization. This is some of the most important work being done in Indigenous communities and is central to their vibrancy and resilience.

of the most important work being done anywhere: In working to revitalize their languages and thus revitalize their cultures, they foster that which makes them human, that which strengthens their life ways, and that which values their very essence and supports their nations.

Because of this, rather than thinking about Indigenous languages as becoming extinct, as long as these extraordinary efforts are being made to revitalize languages, we may think of these ancestral languages, even those with very few native speakers, as sleeping. These significant efforts throughout Indigenous communities, then, aim to wake these sleeping languages.

STRENGTHENING YOUR LINGUISTIC ASSETS

As explained, you are entering postsecondary education with some linguistic capital already. This might include fluently speaking your heritage language(s) and dialects of your home community. We know that this is more likely if you grew up in a family and community that valued these languages and dialects. Recognize that you will find opportunities to revitalize the language(s) of your ancestors or strengthen those that you speak while attending postsecondary education.

We also know that you may not, for many reasons that are not your fault nor that of your family, speak your heritage language. It could be that you lived in a community where the English language completely dominated social interactions. It could be that the social history of your cultural group is such that you do not know your heritage language. It could be that languages other than English were disparaged. It could even be that your family refused to teach you your heritage language because of their experiences—perhaps being punished for speaking their home language in schools and other public places—and they sought to protect you from suffering similar negative consequences.

We cannot emphasize enough that any limitations in your ability to speak your ancestral language is not your fault. We have pointed out that, for the most part, the policies and practices of schools have valued English, and only English. This was all part of efforts aimed at cultural and linguistic assimilation and forced conformity to the dominant language and culture.

Strengthening Your Language Assets on Campus

As mentioned, you can find opportunities to strengthen your linguistic capital and related assets in a postsecondary setting. There are also some things you can do beyond a postsecondary setting to advance your emerging language assets.

Most postsecondary settings, especially those at the community college and university level, will have a modern and foreign languages department. You can pursue classes in any of several languages (Chinese, Japanese, German, French, Spanish, Arabic, etc.). You may also find that, beyond taking classes, you can earn a minor or major degree in those languages. If a minor or major is something you want to actively pursue, be sure the postsecondary institution where you are applying has a degree in the language you are interested in. Note that these departments also may sponsor a lecture or film series to increase opportunities to develop emerging language assets.

On a related note, most colleges and universities have an international studies program, potentially even a minor or major. Those programs may have courses that provide an opportunity to explore issues (health, education, politics, etc.) with an international lens. They might have study-abroad opportunities. The opportunity to travel abroad is often rich in opportunities to strengthen your language assets.

> **PRO TIP:** Consider taking classes in modern and foreign languages departments for many languages or within certain ethnic studies departments to learn about languages taught outside of modern and foreign languages, such as certain Indigenous languages. These classes are a good way to get an initial, basic understanding of the language of interest.

Student clubs focused on a specific language (for example, Spanish Club, Asian American Student Association) offer activities led by students, such as a coffee hour at the Arabic Club. Some ethnic-specific student clubs will encourage the use of one's heritage language. Relatedly, connecting with international students may provide additional opportunities since these students are often open and proud to share their home languages.

Strengthening Language Assets Off Campus

There are often opportunities to strengthen your language assets off campus as well. It might be a renewed interest in speaking your heritage language when you return home to your family and community. Sometimes community centers or organizations offer courses in the languages important to their heritage communities. You can strengthen your language skills by watching programs, listening to podcasts, and reading literature in your heritage language.

Recognizing the value of linguistic assets as described in this chapter, it is never too late to work on recapturing and awakening the language of your ancestors—and you will never regret the efforts you make to do so.

Language is a significant part of one's sociocultural identity, because language and culture are so intertwined. Affirming one's cultural and ethnic identity requires that one also affirm their linguistic identities.

The United States has a long history of undermining languages other than English. While some languages—world languages—have a continual source of speakers of those languages (such as Spanish, Chinese, Portuguese, etc.), other languages are endangered because the number of speakers of those languages are so few. Extraordinary efforts are required to keep these languages alive and vibrant.

We encourage you to learn and use your ancestral language(s). At the same time, when and where possible, make an extra effort to expand your linguistic assets including languages, registers, communication styles, and dialects.

Our ability to use (multiple) languages and their related forms plays an instrumental role in sustaining ourselves through our daily living. It is a primary tool that connects us to our friends, families, and communities. It helps us to learn, to think, and to feel. Likewise, language is a vital asset that helps us share who we are and who we want to become.

Our language, like our sociocultural background, is central to who we are, to our identities. The Chicana feminist writer and scholar Gloria Anzaldúa (1999) wrote: "So if you want to really hurt me, talk badly about my language. Ethnic identity is twin skin to linguistic identity—I am my language. Until I can take pride in my language, I cannot take pride in myself" (p. 81).

END OF CHAPTER ACTIVITY: BUILDING YOUR LINGUISTIC ASSETS

1. Take stock of your current language assets. How many different languages do you know? How many different dialects do you use? Where do you use them? As you think about languages and dialects you can speak, how would you rate your ability to use them: from fluently to hesitantly?
2. Interview someone in your family who speaks a language or dialect other than English. What was their experience learning that language or dialect? What do they say about that language/dialect and their identity? How were they treated, positively or negatively, when speaking that language/dialect? What advice do they have for you about learning and speaking that language/dialect?
3. Ask yourself what languages you want to use fluently. Develop a plan of action related to how you will learn and strengthen those languages during the time you are in postsecondary education. Note which of those actions can be done while on campus and which ones you will pursue off campus, either in the local community or in your home community.
4. Develop a plan for responding to someone who asks you or someone in your presence to speak (standard) English. What would you say to them? How could you push against them in a good way?

SIX

Familial and Social Capital
Walking the Path . . . Together

As the summer draws to a close, Josephine, Anna, Teew, Kieran, and Pancho make plans to have one more meal together before they go their separate ways for the upcoming school year. They realize how much they'll miss each other and want to figure out how to stay connected while they are all off at different schools and even different parts of the state and region.

Over burgers and fries, the friends talk about what they have been up to after completing their ethnic studies class. As they start to have dessert, they talk about orientations they'll need to attend at their respective schools and all the different lists they have been given of things they should make sure to bring to college. There seem to be different checklists for things for their dormitory rooms, things for their classes, and things to bring for registration. One thing they all realize, whether they are moving away for college or staying in town to attend college, is how much they will miss seeing each other and their families on a regular basis.

- While finishing up her ice cream sundae, Josephine shares how much she's going to miss being connected to her home community and cultural clubs she's a part of in town. One thing she was most proud of was being the president of the Black Students Union in high school and her leadership in this club. She has concerns about going to a university that is predominantly White and worries if she'll be able to connect to any clubs or organizations that are like the ones she has had in high school and in town.

- Anna explains how excited she is to have already been connected to an Indigenous Students Organization, or ISO, at her postsecondary institution. There's a meeting of this group for first-year students during orientation, and she already has this event in her calendar. She has heard from some friends a few years ahead of her at the institution that the ISO has been really welcoming and supportive of first-year students. One of her friends has said that the ISO is one of the main reasons they've stayed in college despite different struggles they've faced during their time away.
- Teew is excited for Anna and asks her to make sure to keep in touch with what she learns about this organization and how it helps her with her first year. Teew is still uncertain about whether postsecondary education is the right path for him, but he decided to enroll in a small 4-year college a couple towns away. He knows that being connected to other groups could be a really important thing for him.
- Kieran shares how nervous he is to start orientation week and then classes at the technical college he's attending, but he is so thankful for all the parties and get-togethers his relatives have thrown for him for graduation and now in the last couple of weeks as he prepares to start classes. Kieran is also thankful to his parents, grandparents, uncles, aunts, and chosen family who have always been supportive both financially and emotionally as he's moved through high school, and now as he heads to college.
- Pancho, too, is thankful for all the close connections he has had to family in town and all the ways he's been connected to Latinx people in the community. He feels fully connected to his ethnic, cultural, and linguistic roots, and wonders what it will be like to go to a new part of the state where he doesn't know anybody yet.

As they look at the bill and figure out how much each one of them owes, the five friends realize how fortunate they have been to be tied so closely together through high school and to have had the support of family and friends throughout. These social supports and connections have helped them navigate and complete high school.

As they face the next chapter of their lives, they worry about what might happen with these family connections as they move away from home for the first time and also how they can begin to form new friendships, connections, and networks when they first arrive on campus. They are nervous, but hopeful that the foundational support they already have in their lives will help them in the first few months of their postsecondary education. They realize too that they all have their own individual gifts, assets, and resources that can help other students, like they've helped each other, and they look forward to becoming part of networks of support for other people once they arrive on campus.

INTRODUCTION TO FAMILIAL AND SOCIAL CAPITAL

Making sure we are connected to other people can be one of the most powerful things we do in our lives. Strong family connections can be important sources of help and support, as can the connections we make with people we meet at school, like classmates, teachers, librarians, counselors, and other school staff, who can help us navigate and be successful in postsecondary educational settings. We can also connect to other people in our lives outside of school by engaging in activities like playing sports, taking piano lessons, joining a choir, and being part of youth groups in our communities or at places where we worship, pray, or meditate.

Sometimes these connections are most powerful when we have ties with others both in school and out of school (for example, being connected to a classmate at school, but also being connected because your families go to the same place to pray and meditate). The connections you make in this kind of situation are even stronger because you can connect with that person and their family on multiple levels.

Being connected to others helps us feel supported, seen by others, and appreciated for our contributions to the places we live, work, and study.

In this chapter, we will take a closer look at ways of being more closely connected to other people in our lives. We will learn about two forms of capital: familial capital and social capital. These forms of capital can be powerful ways of engaging with others and finding systems of support for success in school, in work, and in our communities.

EXPLORING FAMILIAL CAPITAL

In this book you have been learning about different forms of capital that can help you navigate postsecondary educational settings. Thus far, we have described and discussed aspirational capital as well as cultural and linguistic capital and the ways in which you can rely on these types of capital to help you thrive in postsecondary education. As noted, you have been accessing different forms of capital throughout your life to help you succeed and achieve in school. We now focus on another form of capital called familial capital.

In the Introduction we used the following description of *familial capital*: "The cultural knowledge nurtured among *familia* (kin) that carries a sense of community history, memory, and cultural intuition." Given this description, you can see that familial capital grounds us as humans. It gives us a sense of belonging, a sense of "who we are" as individual and cultural beings, a sense that we matter, and a sense of what it means to be in and of the world. These are fundamental to being successful wherever you might find yourself.

Familial capital refers to the resources you can access as a result of being a member of your immediate family (the smallest family unit to which you belong) and your extended family (the largest family unit often consisting of grandparents, uncles, aunts, cousins, etc.). The value of familial capital can be seen in the human and personal resources, as well as the social and networking resources, you can access because of family connections to help support yourself in postsecondary education and in society more generally. Immediate families and extended families, then, can provide you support in navigating different structures at school, in local community settings, and at the workplace by providing access to different resources.

These supports can be seen explicitly in the ways in which family members can connect individuals to teachers or decision-makers in schools who can provide new, important information and help individuals understand policies and procedures, especially in new and unfamiliar surroundings.

Sometimes benefits that come from social capital are not so direct. For example, one of the authors recalls the way in which a colleague talked about how members of their family always spoke about the importance of going to school and finishing their degrees in order to have opportunities in one's future career. His colleague's parents used to say you can either "work with your brain or work with your hands and back. Which one would you rather do?" In this case, the parents were trying to point out to their children the physical realities of doing work that required manual labor and the ways in which education could open other forms of work for their children that were not so physically taxing and exhausting.

Similarly, another colleague talked about how his parents always looked forward to report card time. His parents looked closely at the results of the report cards with their children and always showed pride and interest in how their children were performing in school. These parents also looked at perfect attendance as a marker of success and always highlighted the importance of showing up every day to do one's best in school, in life, and in one's workplace. These parents never once talked about college directly, but overall these conversations helped their children develop a mindset of always doing one's best and a work ethic that would be helpful for postsecondary education.

An Extended Example: Familial Capital

Consider the example of two sisters who go to the same high school. Maria is 17 years old and has been at Central High School for 2 years and is in her junior year. Elena is 14 years old and is a freshman at Central High School and just arrived in the United States the summer before her freshman year.

Maria moved to the United States from Mexico 3 years before her sister and so has had time to learn academic English, acclimate to a new school system in the United States, make friends, and find activities at school that she enjoys. A week into the new school year, Elena comes home to share her worries (on many levels) with her family. She knows informal English and feels comfortable with simple conversations with new people, but she has never had to read, write, and speak in English in a school setting. Elena also doesn't know any people in her classes and doesn't feel very welcomed by the people she meets.

Elena has the support of her entire family (her mother, father, uncles, and aunts in the United States and back in Mexico), who remind her often about the importance of education and their support of Elena and of all the children in the family so that they might succeed in school. Elena's parents, uncles, aunts, and grandparents have always shared stories and beliefs with their children about how much they want their children to succeed in school, about the long tradition of valuing education, and the importance of education to one's future success. These family narratives or *consejos* prove to be powerful reminders to Elena of the importance of education and also remind her about the people in her family who support her and who have created opportunities for her to be successful in school.

Fortunately for Elena, she can also rely upon the specific support, advice, and knowledge of Maria, her older sister, in many ways. Maria went through the same period of adjustment 3 years ago and faced different difficulties and obstacles. As the fall term continues Maria provides Elena with strategies for learning English, for making new friends, and for finding her way as a new student at a high school in the United States.

As you can see, having the support of her older sister, and being a member of a larger network of familial support and capital helps Elena navigate the obstacles she might face in high school and helps her have a more positive and successful set of school experiences overall.

> ***Think Alone/Think Together:*** What are the different ways in which you are supported by different forms of familial capital in your family? Do you have brothers, sisters, aunts, uncles, parents, or grandparents who help provide you with the motivation and support to continue in school? Do they help you understand school systems based upon their own experiences in school?

As you think about your familial assets, we encourage you to also think of other people in your life who might support you in significant ways; they might not actually be related to you, but they may act like members of your family in many ways. For example, one of the authors' parents immigrated to the United States from the Philippines when they were in their 20s. They eventually met, got married, and started a family. But because they were the first ones in their family to immigrate to the United States, they did not have many people to connect with from the Philippines. They eventually found connections with other recent Filipino immigrants who became like titas (aunties) and titos (uncles) and de facto caregivers and supporters of their children. These found family members are still important supporters to this day.

EXPLORING SOCIAL CAPITAL

Another form of important capital that we identify is social capital. *Social capital* can be seen in the different ways in which a person can access information about school settings through connections with peers and other social contacts. Through the different networks of people you meet in life, you can begin to connect with a broader range of people (peers, teachers, counselors, community members) who can provide you access to different information and resources you may need to become successful in postsecondary education and in other endeavors in your life.

These networks of people are also extremely valuable to have because they can provide you with important forms of social and emotional support, especially as you navigate through your postsecondary educational experience. For example, as demonstrated in the above example of Elena, some researchers (see, for example, Franquiz & Salazar, 2004) have studied how Latine parents, aunts and uncles, and other family members use *consejos*, or cultural narratives, to share positive feelings, perceptions, actions, and responses about the educational system. It is through these *consejos* that students begin to understand, then internalize, these same feelings about school, their teachers, and the power of education to shape their lives.

Connection to others through these networks and the social capital they provide is important because it is through these relationships that we can learn more about the world around us and about the lives of people who might be different from us. We can expand both the ways in which we have friends from outside our initial close circle, and the ways in which we think about the world we all live in by engaging in conversations and longer-term relationships with new friends, fellow classmates, and future colleagues.

You can utilize these social assets in school, in community settings, and in workplace settings in general. For example, you can call on your social capital as a way to learn more about how to apply to and enroll in a postsecondary institution and also how to navigate that postsecondary institution once you are accepted. Once you start looking carefully and closely, you can start to see how social capital has worked in different forms in your own experience in school.

An Extended Example: Social Capital

Let's return to the example of Maria (the older sister) and Elena (the younger sister) from the previous section on familial capital. Let's fast-forward 4 years. Maria is now a junior in a city college near where her family lives. Elena is planning to attend the same city college. Though both Maria and Elena had difficulties initially adjusting to life in high school in the United States, both eventually succeeded in their classwork, made friends in the classroom and via sports and clubs, and graduated from high school.

Elena is about to start her first year of college in the city in which they live, but again has worries about being able to succeed. During the orientation for first-year students at her college, Elena meets Julia, an advisor who works in the central advising office. Julia is the first person in her family to go to college and understands many of the struggles and questions Elena has as she begins her first few weeks of college. Elena opens up to Julia about all the concerns she has about her first year and Julia offers to meet with Elena every other week to help her with advising, resources, and support.

Through this connection with Julia, Elena can learn about many different resources through which she is able to succeed during her first years in college. As one example, when Elena first starts taking classes at the city college, Julia provides her a list of classes Elena should take to meet some of the initial graduation requirements. She gives Elena recommendations of faculty to take for these courses based upon her experiences and the feedback she has received from other students she has worked with over the years.

Julia encourages Elena to join clubs and sports teams to broaden her circle of friends and find other ways to get involved in school besides going to classes. In this way, Elena is immediately connected to a network of teachers, friends, and other students who can support her right away and provide her advice and good counsel during that important first year of college.

It should be noted here that often the connections one can make via social capital can help to make the other forms of cultural capital you have stronger. When Elena joins the different sports and academic clubs Julia has recommended she learns about classes she should take in her second year and possible careers she can enter once she completes her course of studies.

Elena begins to feel more connected to the classes she has taken, other students she meets in her classes, and to her future career through these initial connections she had made through her social capital networks. She begins to see the importance of earning her college degree and the different career and life pathways it will open for her once she graduates.

We add that a person's experiences with social capital can take various forms. For example, hearing that Elena is looking for a part-time job, Julia might introduce her to the manager of the college bookstore. This introduction might lead to a job offer for Elena to work part-time at the bookstore. This part-time work can help Elena raise enough money to pay for her monthly living experiences and thus help her complete her degree. Through this part-time work, Elena will also get a chance to meet a whole group of new people and friends who can help ground her to campus life at her college.

We also encourage readers to think about the ways that you can and should plan to provide support, encouragement, and access to resources to others in college. In the example above, Julia supported Elena by meeting with her frequently for advising sessions, helping her strategically take courses with specific instructors to help her have a successful experience in college, and connected her to employment opportunities. As she moves forward and finds success, Elena should consider how she can support others that she meets in the same ways she was supported. In this way, Elena can help build up others on their own paths toward success in college and honor the efforts people made to help her be successful.

> **Think Alone/Think Together:** What forms of social capital do you have in your life? Who are the people in your life that connect you to other resources that help you with thinking about school and future postsecondary life? Who are the people in your life who can provide you wise counsel and good advice about what next steps you can take in school, in college, and in your career? How do they lift you up and support you, even when things appear to be tough, or you face particular challenges?

THE IMPORTANCE OF FAMILIAL AND SOCIAL CAPITAL IN POSTSECONDARY EDUCATION SETTINGS

So far we have talked about how familial and social capital work and the ways in which you have had access to these forms of capital during your years in school. As you begin preparations for postsecondary education, it is important to think more specifically about the different challenges you might encounter and how you can use your familial and social assets to work through these challenges.

Completing high school is an important milestone. You have completed the required coursework, attended thousands of hours of classes, laboratory sessions, and homeroom periods, and completed all the requirements for attendance and exams. However, going on to postsecondary education can present different forms of challenges including possibly moving away from your home community and your family for the first time, connecting to a whole new set of students and teachers who are not from your home community, and trying to understand new schedules, testing requirements, and the fees and tuition required for staying in school. In short, postsecondary education is a lot!

Relying on your familial and social capital can be a key factor in finding success in school, staying in school, and finding enjoyment during the entire experience. Returning to the example of Elena, she initially struggled to understand the new structures and systems at her community college, but she made sure to connect right away with her older sister Maria for advice and suggestions on classes and instructors. Because she had to start paying school fees and tuition, Elena also talked to her sister about finding part-time jobs and applying for and accessing scholarships. Elena eventually found part-time work as a lab assistant for one of the chemistry professors. Through this work she became more interested in chemistry and chose it as her major. During her last year of community college, she applied for and received a scholarship designated for students majoring in chemistry at a local university.

Elena then relied upon connections and advice provided by people within her family (familial capital) to connect to other people at the community college who helped her find resources to pay for and complete her community college studies (social capital). The role of family and familial capital is

> **PRO TIP:** It is useful to see your time in postsecondary education as an exercise in relationship-building. The relationships you will build during your postsecondary schooling will serve you well throughout the remainder of your life.

key. At one point, Elena considered dropping out of school. However, after talking to her aunties and uncles, she was reminded of all the barriers and obstacles she had faced in moving to the United States, starting high school, and eventually applying to college. Her aunties and uncles reminded Elena that they believed in her and wanted her to succeed in school.

As this extended example shows, familial and social capital are important because you can rely upon them during times of difficulty or uncertainty. These forms of capital provide clear networks of support that you can call on and connect to when you face obstacles or challenges.

Your education happens in the context of interactions with others in a social setting. When you enter a classroom to start a new class, you are presented with many different opportunities to learn from your teachers, from your fellow students, and from others connected to the postsecondary educational setting, including counselors, advisors, and other support staff.

As you move through higher education, you are also learning how to be a person in the world, how to engage with others, how to relate to others, how to connect to others, and how to communicate and advocate for yourself. These social aspects of education provide you with opportunities to learn more about yourself as a person and about all the tremendous gifts and talents you bring not only to the classroom but to the world. By learning these things about yourself, you also learn to be more fully human and present in classroom settings. These social interactions, in addition to academic learning, provide important foundational experiences from which you get the opportunity to learn who you are as an individual.

Social skills and the ability to connect with other people are important assets to have as you move from postsecondary education into the work world. Employers look for employees who can connect with others on a team, work collaboratively, and create positive, supportive working environments. Accordingly, it is important to take advantage of opportunities to build your social assets and networks during your postsecondary educational experience.

We also encourage you to make your time in postsecondary education as enjoyable and as fun as possible. During your time in higher education, there's a good chance you will make lifelong friends you will stay connected with for the rest of your life. Having friends and connections to students from your classes, your workplace, the clubs you join, and the activities you will participate in will help you to feel connected and grounded. This is especially important if your enrollment in a postsecondary institution requires you to move away from your family and your home community.

Make sure to focus on connecting to friends and teachers who can lift you up while you are in school and be of great support to you when you need it. It's the quality of these networks that matters, not the quantity of friends and supporters with whom you can connect.

> **PRO TIP:** When you arrive on the campus of your postsecondary institution, take a few days to learn about all the services available to help support you. Often these services are located in a Student Services Division or Department of your institution. Keep information about these services in a place that is easily accessible (e.g., notes in your phone) to make it easier to contact staff in these departments when you need additional support. If you happen to get a paper brochure about these services, keep a folder where all this information is available to you when you need it in the future.

We hope you realize that through your educational experiences and your explicit efforts at connecting to familial capital and to building strong social networks, you can change the conditions of your own life. Know that there are people in schools, whether they be your future classmates or teachers, who are just waiting to be helpful and of support. Some people, like college advisors or tutors, are literally being paid to be helpful. That is their job! Find access to these people as you make your way through higher education and lean in to their willingness and desire to want to be of help and support to you.

YOUR FAMILIAL AND SOCIAL CAPITAL: PITFALLS AND CAVEATS

So far, we have focused on the different kinds of familial and social capital assets you can bring to postsecondary education as an individual. However, we want to pause here and clearly acknowledge that there might be times when your assets are not acknowledged or publicly valued by teachers or classmates at school. There might be times when this devaluation of your assets and of your personhood might lead you to feel disengaged from school, from your friends and classmates, and possibly from your family as well. This disengagement might lead you to do poorly in school academically or socially and may cause you to feel like you want to drop out of higher education.

What do you do when you feel ignored at school or dismissed or when you face individual forms of bias, prejudice, or discrimination at the individual level or when out in public with a larger group? What do you do when a fellow student disparages your identity or cultural group? What happens when a professor shows bias or prejudice in a classroom setting?

The roadblock then is not just the treatment you are facing from others, but also not knowing how to handle this potentially racist act or discriminatory act and also your ability to find support to help you when it is needed.

We present two case studies, or stories, that illustrate what we have seen when students face roadblocks that they need to overcome. These cases are based upon our actual experiences working with students in schools. In each case study we present the situation in which the roadblock might occur and then provide some suggestions for you to consider as you think about how you might respond if this were happening directly to you.

Case Study #1

The situation. You attend a higher education institution about 4 hours from your family and home community. You are very close with your mother, father, and siblings and were homesick your first year of classes. By the end of your first year, you figured out a schedule that allowed you to get home once or twice a month to connect with your family. You had developed a close network of friends from your classes and from your part-time work at the college library.

In your second year you receive some terrible news. Your father was in a car accident and requires round-the-clock help and support from members of your family. You begin to travel home more often than you did your first year to help your father and your family and you start to fall behind with classwork and assignments. During one weekend you are at home, your father has to enter the hospital, so you stay with him and your family through part of the following week. You miss a scheduled exam for one of your classes.

Once you return to campus, after your first class meeting for that course you try to talk to the instructor about the exam you missed. The instructor takes out the syllabus for the class and points to the section that refers to late and missed work. The instructor highlights the section that says students must make arrangements with the instructor in advance of any late work or else possibly receive zeros for any assignments they miss. You walk away from class that afternoon feeling deflated. You have been trying to support your father and family at home and now you might receive zeros for missed assignments and the exam. You realize this might endanger your grade for the entire semester and worry about what to do next.

Possible Ways to Respond to the Situation. Here we provide some suggestions for responding in this scenario.

- Instructors in your classes chose to work in postsecondary institutions because they want to help students succeed. Be sure to make every effort to explain to your teacher what is happening in your life and at home. Explain your situation, what your plan is for making up the work, and the timeline you propose for making up the work.
- Make an appointment with your instructor to talk during their office hours so you have more time to explain what is happening and more time for them to ask you questions. When you initially approached the instructor after class, perhaps they were in a hurry to get to their next class or another meeting and didn't have time to fully process your situation. Instructors' office hours provide more time for you to share information and ask for support.
- At your postsecondary institution there will be different support services in place to help you navigate certain situations. You may have an advisor for your discipline that you can meet with. Perhaps

the advisor can help you work on communicating with your instructors to obtain some extensions on your deadlines through the next few weeks. You might get some breathing space to be present for your family (which is crucially important) and still complete your assignments for the term (which is also very important).

- Returning to the ideas we presented at the beginning of the chapter on social capital, what are some ways you can rely upon your friends in class to help you through this current situation? How can you ask them to help support you even while you might have to miss some additional classes? Perhaps you have some peers in class you can meet with regularly to review notes for class meetings you missed. You might be able to have study sessions together to review material you do not understand from just studying the textbook or readings. Lean into support from peers in class who can help you move through this time. In turn, make sure to be of support to peers in class should they ever need help from you in the future.

Case Study #2

The situation. You are in your second year of an apprenticeship training for a technology career. You have been in a relationship with a fellow classmate you met during your first year of the program. Things were going well in the relationship. You enjoyed spending time together, you had mutual friends who were also in the program, and you even took classes together, which was a fun experience. However, between your first and second year of the program, your relationship takes a turn.

The person you were in the relationship with begins to be abusive toward you verbally. You try to talk to the person about the situation, but nothing seems to change. In fact, things became worse in terms of the hurtful things the person says to you. The strain in the relationship begins to affect your academic performance in your program. You do not want to go to classes where you will see that person and you stop turning in assignments. In the middle of the fall term, one of your advisors emails you and asks to meet with you about your academic performance. The advisor provides you with your mid-term reports and says that she is worried you are going to fail your courses and then be asked to leave the program. In addition to the problems with your academic performance, you begin to feel lonely and isolated by this situation. Friends that you had in common now seem to be taking sides and are not returning your text messages or making plans to hang out outside of class.

Possible Ways to Respond to the Situation. We offer the following considerations to address what has occurred in this scenario.

- We realize that this situation can be a very difficult and challenging one. There are emotions involved in any relationship, and there is a sense of loss when you have been closely connected with someone and then there is a break in that connection.
- Know that you are not alone in this type of situation. Remember that you do have friends and family at home who can help support you, friends at the school you are attending who can help you, and support advisors at your institution who are specially trained and who want to help support you.
- Returning to the idea of familial capital, always remember that you have different kinds of support systems available to you. One important form of support is the advice and support you can access via your family and close friends at home. Sometimes having the perspective of someone who loves you and is also not part of the immediate situation allows you to develop ideas and strategies for moving forward that you, immediately in the situation, do not see.
- Although you may have some friends who chose the side of your ex and are not immediately showing up for you, make sure to reach out to friends whom you are still close to. Sometimes what you need is someone just to talk to and process with. Sometimes your close friends can provide ideas and strategies that they themselves had to use in similar situations they've faced.
- Also, know that there are student support services in place at your institution designed to help you, some specifically designed to help you in times of emergency and stressful situations like the ones presented in this case study. For example, many campuses provide

students with specialized support services including emergency and crisis counseling services, health and well-being services, and counseling and psychological services. These services are often provided at no cost to students and staffed with caring, professional staff and counselors trained to make sure you are safe, and to help you think through difficult situations you might face in school; they want to see you be successful.
- We realize that there will be times where you feel alone and isolated, but please always remember that you are not alone, so make sure to reach out to others for help and support. Connect to your family, connect to your friends, and connect to support services specifically designed to help you work through major issues and situations you face in your life. Although your initial inclination may be to retreat from the situation and work through things by yourself, make sure to lean into the support systems and friends and family who want to be there for you and support you through any tough times you may face.

> ***Think Alone/Think Together:*** What are some roadblocks you have faced in your own life? What are some creative strategies you've used to work through, work around, and potentially deconstruct those roadblocks?

IDEAS FOR STRENGTHENING AND EFFECTIVELY USING FAMILIAL AND SOCIAL CAPITAL

Let's be honest: Being Indigenous Students and Students of Color (ISOC), especially if you attend a predominantly White institution (PWI) can be a particularly alienating experience. It can be difficult. It can be challenging. Sometimes you may feel disconnected and isolated. Some of your experiences may make you feel like giving up. What we have tried to provide in this chapter and throughout the book is a real and honest assessment of what it can look and feel like.

Despite these real challenges, attending a postsecondary institution can open up many doors and can provide a range of opportunities and valuable experiences in both the short and long term. Therefore, to plan ahead for possible challenging times, we encourage you to think about how to proactively create systems of support for yourself so that you can build a network of people who can celebrate with you during times of success and accomplishment and who can "have your back" and sustain you during times of struggle and challenge.

Below are some strategies for building your support network at your postsecondary institution, while also continuing to connect to the network of family, friends, and other supporters in your home community.

- When you first arrive on the campus of your postsecondary institution, look to see what clubs and organizations might connect you to your home culture and community. For example, perhaps your family is closely connected to the Korean immigrant community in your city. During your childhood, you spent a lot of time at home with family and close family friends deeply connected to and committed to learning Korean cultural traditions, ceremonies, and celebrations. You regularly went to the Korean cultural center to take language lessons. When you move away to school, we encourage you to look for clubs and organizations either on or off campus that would allow you to continue to build upon that foundation and expand it.
- It may be that your postsecondary institution does not have a club or organization that fits your interest, or that allows you to connect with your culture and community in ways that are helpful to you. If such clubs or organizations do not exist on your campus, see if you can organize fellow students to start such a club.
- Make sure to search out for other ways to connect to your home culture and language through cultural community connections that you can make off campus. For example, look out for community centers, nonprofit organizations, and cultural festivals that connect you to your home culture and community, especially if you are attending a college that is a predominantly White institution. Connections to these community centers and cultural gathering

places can help you feel at home even though you might be physically many hours away from home.
- See if there are language classes you can take for credit or on an audit basis. In these classes you might connect to students also interested in learning the language. The professors who teach the courses will probably let you know about cultural events on campus or on nearby college campuses. Sometimes professors will pull together groups of students who have a deep interest in the study of a particular language or country and arrange an immersive study-abroad course that you can take for credit and thereby expand your own interests and development.
- At many campuses, there are specific student support services in place to help you. There may be an ethnic student center or multicultural student services office to support students' academic needs and development and for counseling support. These centers are also places where students across campus from different cultural groups can gather, socialize, and learn from one another.

As you develop your connections with your fellow students and instructors make sure you think of the larger strategy we referred to earlier in this chapter: building out your network of friends, supporters, and allies. By expanding your network, you will be able to build upon the social capital you already have. Whenever you need support or perhaps face an obstacle during your time in postsecondary education, you will have built out a network of friends, faculty, and staff members who can help you work through that obstacle, find other resources to help you if you need them, and ultimately help you reach your goal of completing your studies and earning your degree!

Remember too that, as you move through college and postsecondary education, you should always be looking for ways to support others that you meet by providing them helpful advice, guiding them through difficult times, and connecting them to others you know who can be helpful resources. As you yourself progress through postsecondary education, you will learn more, become a valuable member of the community of which you are a part, and be a leader in the different communities with which you connect. You will develop experiences as a vital community leader and contributing member

> **PRO TIP:** Many postsecondary institutions have information fairs for clubs and organizations on campus during the first week of classes or during orientation. All of the clubs are student-oriented organizations and are invited to provide information and talk with prospective new members. Sometimes they have free snacks available and free swag! Do not miss these opportunities to learn about new clubs, meet potential friends, sign up for a club or activity, and walk away with some free food and t-shirts!

of the community who can help others succeed, thrive, and have an overall positive experience in school.

Starting life as a student in a postsecondary educational setting can be a disorienting experience. In your first few weeks and months, you will be trying to learn what your class schedule is, what the expectations of your instructors are, and how you can best study and prepare for the academic work expected of you in and out of class. You can also sometimes feel cut off from the systems of support—family, friends, and mentors—you had while in high school.

In this chapter, we have tried to explain how important familial capital and social capital can be for you as you navigate your life in a postsecondary setting. If you face difficulties at school, we encourage you to remember all the family connections back home that can lift you up and encourage you. People like your mother, father, aunties, uncles, and members of your chosen family want you to be successful in your life. Remember to connect back to members of your family while you are in school and continue to build upon those familial connections, rather than separate from them.

Remember, too, the different forms of social capital you already have in your life and the ways in which you want to purposefully expand your networks of social capital as you continue your life in postsecondary education. There will be many different resources and student-focused support centers available to you at your institution.

As mentioned in the chapter, you will also meet other people, such as advisors or fellow students, who can help you navigate school in general, classes you have to take, and ways to find resources to pay for your continuing education. Make sure to think carefully about how you can access these resources so that you intentionally build an ever-widening network of fellow students, professors, and support staff who know you as a person and are committed to helping you thrive.

As already noted, navigating postsecondary education can be a challenging experience. Perhaps you are currently in a postsecondary education setting and have personal experiences of the challenges already. At the same time, attending a postsecondary institution can also be a life-changing experience and can be filled with tremendous opportunities for growth, personal and intellectual discovery, and an opportunity to meet friends you will keep in touch with the rest of your life! We hope that you actively seek opportunities to grow, meet new people and friends, and develop a robust network of friends that complement all the things you are learning as a student at your postsecondary institution!

In the end, we are reminded that we are interconnected as human beings in many, many ways. As Martin Luther King, the theologian and civil rights activist, wrote in his "Letter from Birmingham Jail" (1963): "Injustice anywhere is a threat to justice everywhere. We are caught in an inescapable network of mutuality, tied in a single garment of destiny. Whatever affects one directly, affects all indirectly" (p. 1).

END OF CHAPTER ACTIVITY: RECOGNIZING AND STRENGTHENING YOUR FAMILIAL AND SOCIAL CAPITAL

In this chapter we have discussed concepts related to familial capital and social capital. For this activity we would like you to think more deeply about these forms of capital and how you are already connected to people in schools and in communities that provide you a strong foundation for your life in a postsecondary institution.

Please complete the different steps listed below. Keep your responses and notes for this section in a folder, notebook, or electronic documents, so that at the end of the book you can use your written responses as a springboard for further action once you formally start your postsecondary studies.

- Find some time in your schedule when you can sit quietly and reflect on all the people who have helped you during your years as a student. These people can be family members, close friends of your family, or people you are connected to through school, through sports teams, and through community organizations you are a part of.
- Write out an exhaustive list of all the people who support you. These can be people you know from your current high school, from middle or elementary school, family members at home, people in your local communities and mosques, churches, and other places of worship and contemplation, and within your friendship or familial groups. Just list the names.
- Then, under each person or group you listed, write a short bulleted list of of the ways in which this person or group supports you. Be as explicit as possible. What kinds of things do they do to keep you going in your life, in your schoolwork, and in your life outside of school? For example, perhaps you have an uncle or aunt who has always been supportive of you. They come to as many of your choir concerts, sports events, birthdays as they possibly can. Perhaps they always ask you directly how you are doing and how they can support you. They might help you financially with school fees or music lessons; maybe they are always there with encouraging words and really listen to you when you need help or guidance.
- Think about intangible forms of support as well. How have the people on this list helped you think positively about yourself? Perhaps some people on your list have taught you about the importance of showing respect. Some families use the Spanish phrase *"Bien educado"* to emphasize for their children the importance of always acting in a respectful way—that you can show you are smart to others by being respectful. The ethic of being respectful is an asset in higher education and important to continue to cultivate and develop this posture of being respectful.

How have people positioned you to be successful in postsecondary education by talking about the importance of having respect for others and for yourself as you move through school and move through life?

- As you think about going to college, think about how these systems of support can continue to be a place of encouragement and restorative energy for you.
- Write down some ways you can think about expanding upon these networks of social capital once you start college. For example, can you get involved in extracurricular clubs where you can find supportive friends or mentors to help you navigate your time in college? As you start classes during your first year of college, can you decide to stay after class meetings or attend your professors' office hours in order to get help with the class you are taking and learn more about that particular field of study?
- Taking this reflection one step further, we encourage you to think about how you can start to become a helpful resource of social capital/familial capital to others. Identify ways in which you can begin to be a form of social capital connection for others in your life and in your own family. What strengths, talents, and unique experiences can you provide other people around you with as a resource?
- If you happen to end up living far from your hometown as you attend higher education, in what ways can you think about contributing to students and younger family members in your local cultural community back home?

SEVEN

Political and Resistance Capital
Speaking Truth to Power

Halfway through their first term, the five friends decide to connect electronically on Zoom. After talking about how much they miss each other and home, but are glad to be off at school, their conversation turns to things that have surprised them since entering postsecondary education.

Josephine starts by talking about how active all the students are on her campus. From climate change to LGBTQIA+ rights, it seems like there is always a protest or vigil going on somewhere on the campus of the school they are attending. Pancho discusses working with a student group trying to provide aid to recent immigrants. Anna speaks about how an organization at her school tried to register every eligible student to vote. She is excited to vote in the next election, although she has no idea whom she'll vote for. Kieran says members of his school's student government recently held a teach-in to help people learn more about the importance of supporting diversity on campus after the Supreme Court's recent affirmative action decision. Teew says that he hasn't seen as much activism where he is, but he has been following some activists on social media and sharing their posts with some of his friends from school.

As they wrap up their Zoom call, they talk about how the activism they're seeing at their respective schools compares to what they saw in their home community growing up. Kieran notes that one of the things that has surprised him is how much he knows about activism and community issues because of things they were involved in during high school and within their community. Like the day almost every kid walked

Political and Resistance Capital

out of their high school in support of Black Lives Matter. All five agree that their home community did a lot to help them know and understand the importance of political activism.

INTRODUCTION TO POLITICAL AND RESISTANCE CAPITAL

Like many major societal institutions, the education system, and in particular the system of postsecondary education in the United States, is extremely complex and fraught with a range of contentious political issues. Some of the arguments around these issues reveal our cultural contradictions at work.

On the one hand, postsecondary education can be a tool of empowerment, liberation, and upward social and economic mobility. In addition to what we described in Chapter 1, the difference in earnings between college graduates and those without college degrees is substantial and continues to grow (Hardy, 2022). College graduates tend to be healthier and less likely to suffer from chronic health problems such as diabetes and high blood pressure. They are less likely to die prematurely as compared to those with only a high school diploma. Such data points are often referenced by those promoting the value of higher education.

Additionally, educational institutions, particularly postsecondary institutions, are places where one can encounter courses that teach history, cultures, and knowledge structures of people and communities that can be sources of empowerment, validation, and strength, particularly for those in marginalized communities. At the same time, education can be a path toward self-actualization and fulfillment. One need only ask the slave who was denied the opportunity to learn to read, or the woman interested in science who was denied the opportunity to be a doctor or an engineer, how important access to education can be in one's life and for one's ability to become one's full self.

Unfortunately, while education can be liberating and empowering, it can also be a tool of oppression and colonization. The history of Native American boarding schools and English-only school requirements are two stark examples of American education policies and practices that highlight the way education can be anything but uplifting and supportive.

Not only have U.S. postsecondary institutions been born out of this contradictory and complex history; they are also part of the complex and often antagonistic present-day political landscape as well. For example, a school might promote and value diversity, equity, and inclusion, while being subject to bans on teaching subjects like critical race theory or gender studies.

Consequently, postsecondary institutions are not neutral teachers and producers (via research) of knowledge. And you as a student are likely to encounter situations where you may need to draw on your political and resistance capital not only to navigate the postsecondary education landscape, but maybe even to play a part in making your institution better: more inclusive, more equitable, more just.

EXPLORING POLITICAL CAPITAL

In this chapter we focus on two additional types of capital or assets that you can rely on to help you successfully navigate and thrive during your time in postsecondary education. The first of these is political capital. *Political capital* refers to assets that allow you to influence the structures, institutions, and situations around you in a way that is positive and advantageous for yourself and for others on whose behalf you are advocating.

Occasions where you might need or want to rely on your political capital can arise in a variety of situations, at different levels, and on different scales. For example, you might have a teacher who assigns a heavy workload or does not make the requirements of an assignment clear. In response, you and a couple of your fellow classmates might attend the professor's office hours and ask her to provide more clarity or to extend the due date. This would be an example of using your political capital, because you would be using your position and power as a student paying for the course to try to influence the situation regarding your class in a way that will hopefully lead to positive changes for you and your classmates. This is an example of using your political capital on a small scale.

However, you might find during your postsecondary career that you want or need to use your political capital to make large-scale changes as well. For example, let's say your institution decides to greatly increase tuition after you enroll without taking into account the impact such an increase might have on students. In response, you could sign petitions, participate in a social media campaign, write an email to your school administration, participate in a march, or engage in a range of other activities geared toward influencing the institution to not raise tuition. This would be an example of using your political capital on a larger scale. These are just two examples of the type of situations where it might be useful and helpful to rely on political capital.

It is also important to note that use of one's political capital need not be confined to addressing situations at one's school. Often, there are local and larger-scale political issues outside of one's institution you may want to be a part of. For example, in the wake of the murder of George Floyd in 2020, many students in postsecondary institutions across the country became involved in protests and demonstrations or called upon their schools and communities to better address the racial issues they faced on a regular basis.

At the same time, use of one's political capital need not always be in response to something negative. Sometimes political capital can be used to keep something positive, or to organize for something good, or to raise awareness of an important issue. Members of the LGBTQIA+ community might organize a series of Pride month events, or Indigenous community members might hold a vigil to raise awareness about missing and murdered Indigenous women.

Effective use of one's political capital can happen through individual acts as well, such as volunteering your time for a charity you care about, or forwarding a message you deem important through social media.

However, as the above examples demonstrate, political capital is often best exercised in collective action with others. Two thousand students protesting a tuition hike is likely more effectively heard, and more likely to elicit the desired response, than a protest by only two students. As a result, you may find that engagement in which you deploy your political capital in concert with others can sometimes be one of the most rewarding and sustaining activities in which you participate. Not only can such engagement lead to positive change and help make your institution more supportive, it can also be a place where you find like-minded people with similar interests, leading to life-long friendships.

At the same time, working in concert with others to better your individual and group situations often provides the opportunity to develop valuable leadership, organizational, and persuasive skills. Skills that will serve you well throughout your life.

EXPLORING RESISTANCE CAPITAL

Closely related to, and often deeply intertwined with political capital, is resistance capital. *Resistance capital* is the "knowledges and skills fostered through oppositional behavior that challenges inequality" (Cuauhtin, 2019a, p. 249). Students from nonmainstream cultures and communities have a long and rich history of resistance upon which to draw.

In fact, much of the political capital and assets that one might possess are often born out of, or deployed as a result of, the use of resistance capital. Rosa Parks refusing to give up her seat on the bus, protestors insisting that Black Lives Matter, demonstrators blocking the building of environmentally harmful pipelines, parents pushing the local school board for bilingual educational opportunities are all examples of the effective use of resistance capital. These examples also show how resistance and political capital often go hand in hand or are two sides of the same coin.

Unfortunately, the complicated history of postsecondary education, together with the current political climate, as noted above, make it likely you will find yourself in situations during your time in postsecondary education where you will want or need to rely on your resistance capital. As with political capital, resistance capital can be used on a small or large scale, individually or collectively. At the same time, the use of resistance capital can sometimes come in the form of a refusal to act or an unwillingness to engage. One of the authors recalls an experience that illustrates this point:

> I had a professor during one of my classes who was always nicer to the White men in the course than to anyone else. One day he called on me and even though I gave him the right answer he proceeded to yell at me in front of the class accusing me of not being prepared. In reality he had made a mistake. I was right and he was wrong. When a fellow student raised her hand and pointed out the mistake, he did not acknowledge that he was wrong, and he certainly didn't apologize. Instead, he just moved on as though nothing had happened.

> I refused to answer another question in that course for the rest of the semester, no matter how many times he called on me, even when I knew the answer. I may have had to take the course to graduate, but I certainly didn't have to fully engage with the professor to pass the course.

When faced with a situation like that described in this anecdote, the desire to resist and disengage can be strong. But it is equally important to be sure that you are using your resistance capital to engage in forms of resistance that are transformational in nature and not self-defeating. As Solórzano and Delgado Bernal (2001) explain, resistance that is based in awareness and critique of the oppressive conditions and structures of one's situation, and that is motivated, at least in part, by a sense of social justice, has the potential to lead to empowering and transformative acts.

The above story helps illustrate how one can use one's resistance capital to manage sometimes difficult situations encountered during one's postsecondary journey. (See Chapter 9 for more strategies on taking care of your health and well-being.) Refusing to engage with and follow the expectations in a course where a student is not being treated well is a form of resistance. In refusing to answer and engage with the professor, the student recognized and acknowledged the unfair and oppressive nature of the situation in which she found herself.

Importantly, her resistance could have come in the form of dropping the class, or in blaming herself for the professor's actions, or in questioning whether she belonged in the educational environment in the first place. Instead, she recognized and acknowledged the discriminatory and oppressive acts of the instructor and took effective action to shield herself from participating in those continued acts. At the same time, she stayed in the course and found a way to persist and eventually earn her degree. Sometimes the most profound and transformational resistive act is to succeed.

The above example also shows how resistance capital can be used in positive and supportive ways as well. The classmate who spoke up in defense of and in support of the student the teacher was berating engaged in an act of kindness, which in itself was an act of resistance. In this scenario, neither student used their political capital, because in refusing to answer any more questions, or in speaking up on behalf of the other student, they were not necessarily looking to influence or change the situation. Rather, both students acted in opposition to and in defiance of what happened in the class. Often, there can be tremendous value to oneself and one's dignity, and it can be affirming of one's humanity, to resist that which one thinks is wrong, unfair, or unjust.

YOUR POLITICAL AND RESISTANCE CAPITAL: PITFALLS AND CAVEATS

Exercising one's resistance capital can be an important tool for not only surviving, but thriving, during your postsecondary journey. At the same time, while using one's political capital can be transformative and empowering, engaging in resistant and political acts can sometimes come at a cost. Unfortunately, such acts can sometimes prove to do more harm than good, or to not be worth the trouble. They might also detract from more useful and positive activities you need to engage in to successfully complete your degree.

Accordingly, it is important to be thoughtful and reflective before using your political and resistance capital, an important step toward taking action; it is reflection plus action that equals **praxis** (Freire, 1970). For example, ask yourself why you might resist or why you might want change in a particular situation. Perhaps make a list of what you might do to resist or make change, and then map out the pros and cons of each action and the likelihood of its success.

Try to be mindful of acts and strategies that might make sense and feel good in the moment, but may be detrimental to you in the long term. For example, you might resist by choosing to no longer attend a particular class where **microaggressions** happen repeatedly, but missing the material offered in class may cause you to be less well prepared for the final exam. In that instance, a different use of your resistance capital might be warranted. Keep in mind also that your very presence on a postsecondary campus, or in a course, can be an effective act of resistance, or a political act. Successfully earning your degree even more so. (See chapter 9 for strategies for dealing with microaggressions and similar situations.)

Political and Resistance Capital

> ***Think Alone/Think Together:*** Chances are, long before you enter postsecondary education you have had experience with using your political and resistance capital. Reflecting on the following questions should help you identify where you have developed and used your political and resistance assets in the past.
>
> - Think of occasions when you felt something was unjust or you wanted change. What, if anything, did you do about it? If you did something about it, how effective were the strategies you used? Why or why not?
> - Have you seen someone in your home community fight for change or resist something they didn't like? What did they do and what was the result?
> - As noted above, being successful, particularly when others do not think you are capable of it, can be an effective use of your political and resistance capital. Think of times when you accomplished something you didn't initially believe you could do, or when others told you that you could not.

STRATEGIES FOR STRENGTHENING YOUR POLITICAL AND RESISTANCE CAPITAL

Knowledge Is Power

Often it is hard to know whether or not and to what extent you can advocate for yourself, or the ways in which you can effectively resist if you do not know what rights you have, or if you do not understand how the institution of which you are a part is structured. Accordingly, one important way to strengthen your political and resistance capital is to become well versed in your rights as well as the rules and procedures of your school.

At the same time, all schools provide avenues through which you can make complaints or bring issues to the attention of the administration. All schools provide a range of helpful and supportive services as well. (See Chapter 8 regarding developing your navigational capital.)

There are a range of both state and federal laws that protect your rights to free speech, fair treatment, and equality more generally. There are laws that provide the right to accommodations and other supports if you have a disability, and that prohibit discrimination based on a range of protected categories such as race and ethnicity, religion, gender, gender identity, sexual orientation, disability, veterans' status, national origin, and similar categories. There are laws, and likely school policies and procedures, that protect your right to *due process* (a fair procedure or hearing and a right to be heard) and that require institutions to provide certain kinds of transparency and records, and that protect your right to privacy as a student.

Most of these policies and procedures can be found on the website for the school you are attending, as can a lot of information about your school in general. Internet searches regarding a particular topic can be an effective way to educate yourself and to find helpful resources as well. Most institutions also provide student advocates, attorneys, or ombudspersons who can help and support you.

In addition to being knowledgeable about your rights and the rules and procedures that might apply in each situation, you can build your political and resistance capital by becoming more knowledgeable and by building your skills more generally. For example, if you find yourself in the position of wanting to argue against a tuition increase, as in one of the above examples, you can more effectively figure out how to do so if you educate yourself about how tuition rates are set at your institution and what your tuition dollars are used for.

Luckily, postsecondary educational institutions offer a range of opportunities for you to learn and strengthen your skills in ways that will help contribute to developing your political and resistance capital. For example, you might take a research paper writing assignment in a course that allows you to pick the topic and focus on an area of interest, such as what are the most effective grassroots organizing strategies. There are often plenty of internship and externship opportunities that will help you develop your knowledge and skills in particular areas as well. Similarly, community groups that do work you are interested in often welcome volunteers.

Effectively advocating for oneself and others requires good oral and written communication skills. Therefore, taking advantage of opportunities that strengthen these skills will not only help you build your political and resistance capital; good communication skills are also important tools for school success and beyond. Developing your voice and being able to effectively communicate your ideas can help you shape and influence the conversations that are important to you, no matter where those conversations might take place.

There Is Strength in Numbers

As noted in the above discussion, one's political and resistance capital is often best utilized in conjunction with others. Accordingly, developing supportive relationships with others who can act in concert with you or support the individual acts in which you might engage is an important component of building your political and resistance capital.

As with opportunities to educate yourself, postsecondary institutions offer many opportunities to make connections and build relationships. Nearly all schools offer affinity groups, centered on a range of personal characteristics such as one's race or gender identity, that are meant to provide safe, supportive spaces for those in marginalized communities.

Additionally, all schools offer clubs and a broad range of student groups where you can find others who are interested and passionate about things of importance to you. It can be helpful and supportive to join such groups, as we have discussed in previous chapters. Working on projects in which the group might be engaged, or taking on leadership roles, can help build your knowledge and skills as well.

One student group that often has the ability to influence change at any institution is the student government. Members of student government often sit on committees and influence important policies and decision-making at their institutions. There are also many community groups you can join as well. As a recent graduate explained to one of the authors:

> During my sophomore year I volunteered at our local soup kitchen. I enjoyed the work and what a difference we made with all the people we helped in our community so much that the next year I obtained a position on their

governing board, and now I have applied to go to graduate school in nonprofit management.

Another place where you can often find help and support is through relationships with the faculty and staff at your institution. In addition to serving as helpful mentors who can help you better understand and navigate the system, they will often advocate on your behalf. They are the people who might be able to make the changes you seek. As a current student conveyed to one of the authors:

> In talking with others in our cohort, a group of friends of mine and I realized that there were many scholarship and internship opportunities that other students were getting that we hadn't even heard about. The other students found out about these opportunities by talking to faculty who they had a relationship with. We complained to our department head about the unfairness. She listened and now all scholarship and internship opportunities are posted on the department website to make sure everyone knows about them.

Take Care of Your Mental and Physical Health

Finally, engaging in situations that require you to use your political or resistance capital can be emotionally and physically difficult and can sometimes make you feel unsafe. Accordingly, it is critical to take care of yourself and to have places where you can be your authentic self and feel secure. More on strategies for doing so can be found in Chapter 9.

While we may all wish for a time in the near future where a book like this one, which focuses on providing support and encouragement for those who come from marginalized communities, will no longer be necessary, we unfortunately are not there yet. This means that you are likely going to encounter situations during your postsecondary educational journey that will require you to tap into your resistance capital and to use some of your political assets to not only survive but to thrive and make your institution a better place.

Whether and to what extent you do so will be up to you, but hopefully the advice provided in this chapter will help you build those assets, so that if and when you might need them they will be available and helpful to you in such a way that you can persist in your studies and achieve the educational success you are working for.

Throughout it all, we are reminded by Cesar Chavez (1984), co-founder with Helen Chavez and Delores Huerta of the United Farmworkers Association, of the importance of political and resistance capital: "Once social change begins, it cannot be reversed. You cannot un-educate the person who has learned to read. You cannot humiliate the person who feels pride. You cannot oppress the people who are not afraid anymore" (p. 7, para 1).

END OF CHAPTER ACTIVITY: BUILD YOUR KNOWLEDGE TO INCREASE YOUR POWER

As noted in this chapter, a key component of building your political and resistance capital is knowing your rights and knowing the procedures and structures of your school. To help you build this knowledge, this End of Chapter Activity invites you to go on an electronic scavenger hunt to help you learn more about the postsecondary institution you might attend. Specifically, once you have decided which school you plan to attend (or even if you are trying to decide between a couple of schools) go to their website and see if you can find the items in the following list. Once you find them, it is recommended that you keep a Word or notes document where you copy the URL for the website so that if needed later you can easily find the necessary information.

Scavenger Hunt List of Items

- Student Code of Conduct.
- Student complaint procedures—where a complaint can be filed, with whom, and with respect to what issues.
- Information on the Diversity, Equity, and Inclusion (DEI) office or similar office focused on equity and inclusion—see where the office is located and what kinds of support and information they provide.

- The Title IX office and complaint procedures, and/or Title IX coordinator (sometimes this person or office is located under the DEI office).
- A student's attorney, a student ombudsperson, or a similar person or group whose job it is to advocate for students and protect their rights.
- Your school's antidiscrimination and antiharassment policies (these could be in the student handbook)
- Information about student government—who the officers are, the standing committees, what projects they are working on, what they do in support of students, how you can be involved in their work if that is of interest to you.
- A list of established student clubs and organizations, what they do, and how you can join.
- Is there a student-run newspaper or magazine? What stories have they carried about the major issues on your campus recently?
- Recent news articles and announcements more generally about your school. These will inform you about the important issues, particularly political ones, that may concern or interest you as an incoming student.

EIGHT

Navigational Capital
Making the Strange Familiar

Pancho, Josephine, Anna, Teew, and Kieran meet for coffee during Winter break after their first semester at their respective universities and colleges.

Pancho: How were your professors? Did you like them?
Josephine: I didn't really talk to them. One of my classes had like 300 students. A couple of my classes had grad student instructors.
Anna: I talked to one of my profs after class. She seemed cool.
Teew: I went to one of my professor's offices. Worst experience of my life.
Pancho: Why? What happened?
Teew: It was for my Indians of the Northwest Anthro class. The prof was talking about Indigenous languages in class like they were a thing of the past. As if nobody spoke them anymore. I thought I'd drop by his office and tell him I could get one of my relatives to come to class to speak a native language in front of the students. My grandmother worked on our tribe's dictionary. She'd love to come speak to the students about our native language.
Kieran: What did the prof say?
Teew: I went to his office and knocked on his door. The professor, who's not Indigenous but he's got all this Indigenous art on his walls, takes forever then says come in. But he doesn't ask me to sit down, he just stares at me and says, "Yeah?" So I say to him, "I have relatives who speak one of the languages you were talking about in class the other day." The professor says, "And?" So, I say, "I could ask one of my relatives to come in. She's worked on our tribe's dictionary. Students can hear the language being spoken." The professor said, "No, that's okay."
Anna: What did you do?

Teew: I left. What else could I do?

Anna: That sucks. If I were you, I'd send an email to the president. Tell him if he's gonna employ racists, you're gonna call them on it. Tell the Native Student Union or a native professor. Get them to help.

Keiran: Just go to class, jump through the hoops they ask you to jump through, and pass the class. You need 4 years and a piece of paper to get a job. No reason to give that prof any reason to eff with your life.

Pancho: Did you tell the prof you were coming to the office? Maybe he was busy or something. You gotta go during office hours. That's why they have them. My prof said she wants us to come during office hours. She just sits around waiting for students to drop by during office hours.

Josephine: That prof is insecure. He doesn't want his authority challenged. He sees your relatives as a threat to his authority. Does the prof speak an Indigenous language? Did you learn any words or any bit of a native language?

Teew: No. I don't think he speaks an Indigenous language. He just had us memorize the "traditional linguistic areas" of Indigenous language families in the Northwest. That was it. I didn't really talk during class. None of the other students said anything or asked about native languages. I don't know about you, but it feels at times like college is a game with a bunch of rules I don't know but everyone else knows somehow. It's a lonely place. I feel invisible.

INTRODUCTION TO NAVIGATIONAL CAPITAL

A common emotion you may encounter as Indigenous Students and Students of Color (ISOC), especially if you find yourself on a predominantly White campus (PWI), is the feeling that you don't know how things work. You may think that other students are familiar with, and take for granted, certain norms, knowledges, or rules that you do not know or are not familiar with about the functions and day-to-day business of the university. Other students, especially White students from privileged backgrounds, may appear as though they have come to campus with an understanding of how higher education functions already uploaded into their minds. They may have already considered answers to these questions:

- When should I visit a professor?
- What majors are offered at the university and what kinds of jobs can I get with them?
- Do I need a minor to graduate?
- What does the registrar's office do?
- Some universities seem to have colleges—do I need to apply to both the university and a college?
- How many credits should I take in a semester or quarter?
- What happens if I cannot fully pay for my tuition? Are there resources to help me?
- What does the chair of a department do?
- What are prerequisite courses?

For many Indigenous Students and Students of Color, the university is a large question mark rather than an open door to the future. Whether or not a university is a question mark or open door has much to do with your navigational capital.

EXPLORING NAVIGATIONAL CAPITAL

Some students come to college with a lot of *navigational capital*: the ability to understand and successfully maneuver through institutions. The more navigational capital a student has, the more they can thrive in an institution because they know how the systems in the institution work and, most importantly, how to make those systems work for them!

Navigational skill within a university entails the realization that most universities, as institutions, were not created with People of Color in mind. Nor were they designed to foster and promote cultural differences, especially the cultures of ISOCs. Often ISOC families have had little or no exposure to postsecondary education and therefore may not have acquired all the navigational capital that families who have had years and even generations of exposure to college can share.

In sum, ISOCs do not often come to postsecondary education with the amount of navigational capital they need to thrive. Accordingly, this chapter is meant to help you build your navigational capital.

STARTING WITH THE BASICS

How are postsecondary institutions staffed? At any postsecondary institution you decide to attend, many of the people you will see and meet on campus won't be students. Rather, they will be working to keep the college running whether that is planning courses and events, working to keep the buildings and classrooms in good condition, or working to keep the college on solid financial footing. Here, in very broad terms, are some of the folks charged with keeping the lights on at postsecondary institutions—both literally and figuratively.

Who Watches Over the University?

The Board of Trustees is a group of people, sometimes alumni of the institution, who meet regularly with the university president and upper administration to make sure the school is running as intended by its founders. The trustees in many public universities are chosen by the state's governor.

University President and Division VPs. Universities are often led by a university president. From there, it is structured in what are called "divisions" with a vice president (VP) in charge of each division. For instance, all universities will have an *academic affairs division* or its equivalent. Most universities will also have a *student services division* and a *budget/finance division*.

Provost. The VP in charge of the academic affairs division in a university is called a provost; this position is responsible for all the schools and colleges within the university.

Deans. Deans oversee colleges or schools within a university. Deans work with assistant deans, chairs, and staff to make sure all the education personnel (students, faculty, staff) and elements related to education (curricula, money/budget) are working toward the common goal of education and graduation. Deans are also in charge of the finances of a college or school.

Figure 8.1 shows the generic structure of a college or university (also known as an organizational chart or org chart) showing the different divisions headed by a VP. Keep in mind that the college or university you are researching may have a slightly different structure. You can search online to find the org chart of your college or university.

Figure 8.1. Generic Organizational Chart

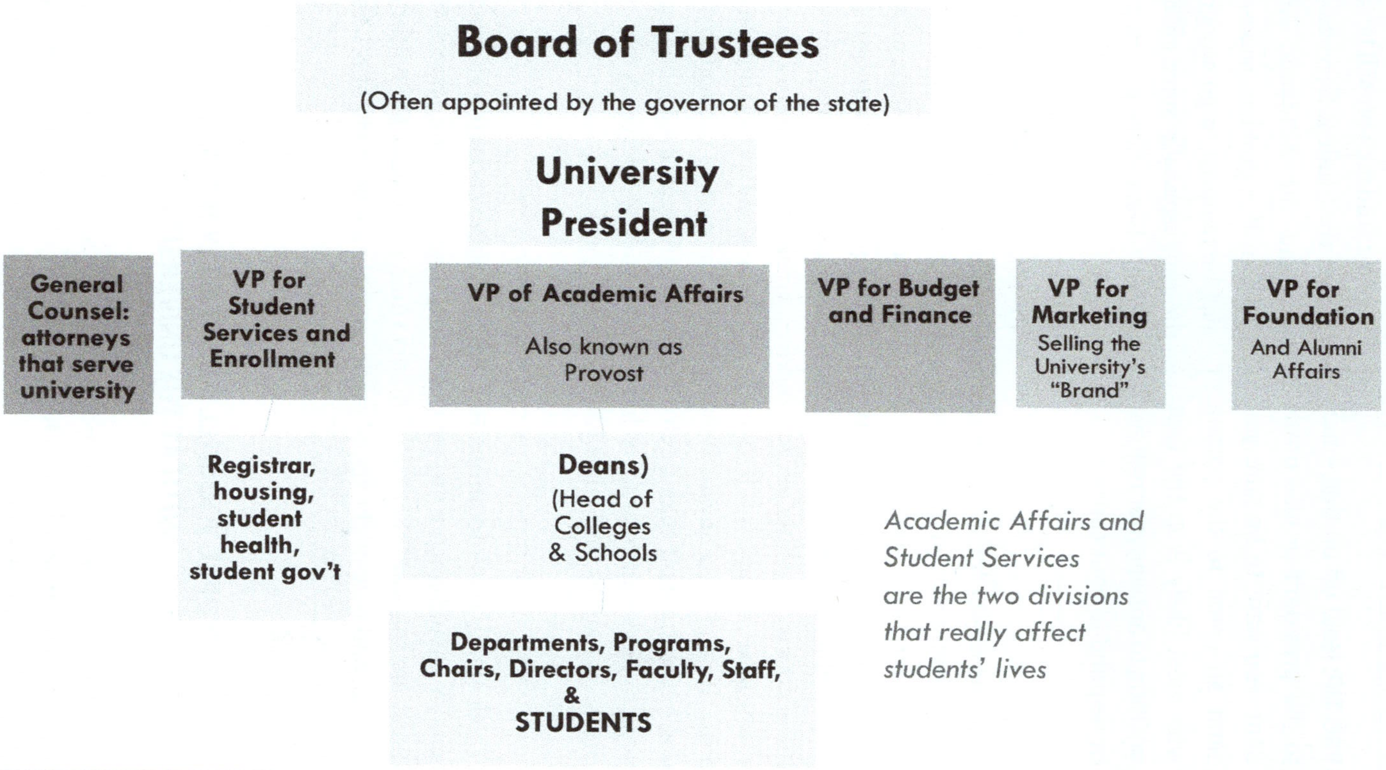

Board of Trustees
(Often appointed by the governor of the state)

University President

- General Counsel: attorneys that serve university
- VP for Student Services and Enrollment
  - Registrar, housing, student health, student gov't
- VP of Academic Affairs
  - Also known as Provost
  - Deans (Head of Colleges & Schools)
  - Departments, Programs, Chairs, Directors, Faculty, Staff, & STUDENTS
- VP for Budget and Finance
- VP for Marketing
  - Selling the University's "Brand"
- VP for Foundation And Alumni Affairs

Academic Affairs and Student Services are the two divisions that really affect students' lives

> **PRO TIP:** Hold off on that email to the president or vice president. You want to be sure you send an email to the person who most likely is in the best position to answer your request or respond to your concern.

As a student, you will be within both the Student Services division and the Academic Affairs division. If a problem arises, you may be tempted to go straight to the top, especially since an email or dm (direct message) on social media is easy to send. We would caution you against emailing the VP for student services/affairs or the VP (Provost) for Academic Affairs, or the university president. You should go to the person most immediately in charge of the problem.

Consider this: If you were a boss and your worker had an issue with you, would you prefer they go above your head to your boss or your boss's boss without telling you? For example, if you have a question about your enrollment in courses or about tuition and fees, email the registrar's office, first checking to see if there is a "frequently asked questions" (FAQ) link on their website. If you have a question about a course or professor, email that professor, or the assistant chair or chair of the department. In case of an emergency, campus security, student health, or a student emergency hotline, if available on campus, should be your first phone call.

> ***Think Alone/Think Together:*** How much of your school life and campus life should you put on social media (Instagram, TikTok, Snapchat)? What are the ways that social media could make your life better at school, and how might social media complicate your life at school?

PEOPLE YOU WILL MOST LIKELY INTERACT WITH AT THE UNIVERSITY

Chairs. Chairs oversee academic departments within a college or school (English Department, Physics Department, etc.). Some departments are so large they have an assistant chair. Chairs work with the professors or faculty of a department to make sure courses are being offered that fulfill requirements for the department major and for graduation. They are also in charge of the finances of the department.

Faculty. There are three general ranks of faculty or professors: Assistant, Associate, and Full. Assistant professors are typically pre-tenured or do not have tenure. **Tenure** is an extended appointment to a college or university. It provides faculty with job security and, as important, the security to address controversial issues without fear of losing their job. In most cases, assistant professors are given 6 years to achieve tenure, or they will be asked to leave the university.

Once a professor achieves tenure, they become an associate professor (which usually includes a salary increase). They can remain an associate professor until they retire if they so desire. However, some professors want to go beyond associate and become full professors. Full professors are tenured professors who have achieved a level of national or regional recognition—usually determined by the university—in terms of publishing, teaching, or years in the position. Their pay is better than associate professors, and there are often other perks that come with a full professorship such as opportunities for leadership advancement and less frequent reviews of their performance.

Graduate (Grad) Students. Master's students, PhD/doctoral students, and students earning advanced professional degrees (doctors, lawyers, etc.) are called graduate students. Graduate students, especially doctoral students, are often offered opportunities to teach at universities while getting their graduate degrees.

Staff. Staff positions differ from university to university and sometimes within colleges and departments at the same university. There will most likely be an office manager in charge of the front desk; a business manager or accountant in charge of the finances and budget; a curriculum or records manager in charge of helping the chair create course schedules; and some departments may even have a staff member who is a student advisor.

One of the first things you should do when you arrive on campus is learn where to receive academic advising. Look for an "academic advising office" or "advising center" or something similar. Academic advising provides guidance on all the things you need to do to meet graduation requirements as well as help exploring academic opportunities (such as a semester abroad). The advising center can break down and explain the differing levels of requirements

> **PRO TIP:** Find the right academic advice and seek it early. Advising is a big part of just about every person's job at the university. So seek out those whose specific job is advising but also those who are "in the know" about how to make things work as well.

within the university (number of credits, types of course requirements, etc.).

The advising office is also a great place to discuss what **majors** the university has to offer, and what requirements may be included in the majors. This is important because some majors have a very structured curriculum (courses students are required to take to complete the degree) and if you do not sign up for the major and begin taking the courses right away, you may have to wait a year for another opportunity.

Head to the advising center early when you get to campus. Once you determine your major, the department your major is housed in should provide you with an advisor who can help guide you through what courses and requirements you need to fulfill to graduate with that specific degree. If you determine that you would like to change majors, the advising center would be a good place to return to as you explore other academic options and opportunities. Note that changing majors might extend the time it will take you to graduate.

What Types of Requirements Might You Need to Complete to Graduate?

Each college and university has its own requirements for you to graduate and receive a degree. A degree, of course, opens avenues into future employment. It is good to know early on what you need to do to graduate—what is *required* of you to get your degree. Most of these requirements come in the form of types of courses you must take, but there is also usually a grade point average (GPA) requirement (above 2.0 is standard). At 4-year colleges and universities there will also be a required amount of upper-division courses you need to take. **Lower-division courses** are classes offered at the freshman level (often these course numbers begin with 100 or 1000) and sophomore level (course numbers 200 or 2000). **Upper-division courses** are classes at the junior (courses begin with 300 or 3000) and senior (400 or 4000) levels.

There are three main types of requirements for the courses you are likely to find at your college or university:

1. *University Requirements:* these are known as *General Education Requirements* or Gen Eds, for short. We describe these more fully below. You can find the Gen Eds online, but it is also helpful to ask the advising center what the Gen Ed requirements are for your postsecondary institution.
2. *Department/Major Requirements:* These will be the requirements for whatever major you choose. Usually, these will be a series of courses, often in your last 2 years, created by the department to give you the credentials and degree you will need to start work after college. Some majors allow for many different classes to fulfill the requirements. Other majors have strict class requirements with little flexibility.
3. *Minor Requirements: You do not need a minor to graduate*, but if you choose to do a minor (and many students do), you will need to take fewer courses in order to complete the minor degree.

General Education Courses/Requirements

If you attend a 4-year college or university, you will often spend the first 2 years completing a series of university-required courses known as **general education requirements** or **Gen Eds** for short. These requirements are also known as Core Courses, Core Curriculum, or University Studies. There are many purposes of these general education requirements, but overall, they are to help students to achieve a well-rounded education in multiple areas: this is known as a *liberal arts* education.

Gen Eds also allow you to take courses from many different departments, programs, and colleges to pique your interest in potential majors and perhaps help you gain an understanding of what you can do after graduation. The courses that make up the Gen Eds at your university have been chosen by faculty and administration (sometimes with student representatives) to fulfill the liberal arts mission of the institution.

> **PRO TIP:** The liberal arts do not have anything to do with American politics. They help make you a well-rounded person and expand your horizons beyond the knowledge and skills that are important for the career of your choice.

A liberal arts education is not the creation of any American political party. In fact, liberal education has its roots in the founding of European universities hundreds of years ago in the Middle Ages. The universities at that time, following Greek thinkers centuries before them, thought that there were seven liberal arts or disciplines necessary for a person to be educated. Those seven were: grammar, logic, rhetoric (persuasive writing), arithmetic, geometry, music, and astronomy.

Today, a liberal arts education at the university usually means every student at the university will have taken courses (Gen Eds) in the formal and natural sciences (such as math and geography, respectively), the social sciences (such as history and ethnic studies), humanities (such as literature and foreign languages), and arts (such as music and drama).

Majors

One of your biggest decisions as a postsecondary student is what your major will be. A major is an area of intensive study often completed during the last 2 years of college, as your first two will be occupied satisfying the Gen Ed requirements. Therefore, you will have your first 2 years to think about what academic discipline you want to focus and major in. This is important because your academic major often leads to the type of careers you would like to pursue.

This means that you do not have to know what you want to do with your life when you start college. You have time to explore majors (and figure out what subjects you feel yourself drawn to), think about your own personal goals, and figure out which major might take you where you want to be after you graduate.

Besides taking classes in different academic programs, another great place to start exploring what you can do with certain majors is to visit a department's website. Department websites, beyond describing the major and minors offered (along with requirements for admission, if any, and graduation requirements), will often have examples of what you can do after you graduate with one of their majors. Department websites may have alumni profiles where you can read about what previous graduates have done with their majors.

> **PRO TIP:** Find the right major for you. A major is the beginning of a pathway for your professional career and, in many ways, will impact future opportunities as well.

Visit the **career services office** or center on campus during your freshman year. Colleges and universities have dozens of different majors. Each major opens potential opportunities for a multitude of different jobs after you graduate. The career services office or center on your campus can help you explore majors and their potential post-graduation opportunities. The career services office can give you information on *career fairs* where potential employers come to campus to seek out students who may be interested in employment after graduation and to share what their companies do and why you might want to apply. Career services offices can also inform you about potential **internships**, which are paid or unpaid positions where companies hire current students for a period of time. You can even get class credit for some internships. Lastly, career services offices often hold resume writing and job interviewing skills workshops and other workshops to help you prepare for life after graduation.

> **PRO TIP:** Finally, make sure to connect with fellow students at the university or others in your program of study. Being just 1 or 2 years ahead of you in their journey they can be rich resources of information about how to apply and get into a specific program or college, which professors and classes are the most engaging and supportive within a program, and how to think strategically about both your coursework, related internships, and career paths after you complete the degree.

Minors

Like majors, minors provide the opportunity to learn more about an academic area of interest but they have fewer requirements to complete. While you do not need a minor to graduate, many students opt to do a minor for professional and personal reasons. Your minor does not have to be related to your major. It can be a personal area of interest. Or, you can earn a minor that enhances your major and might boost an employer's interest. For example, let's say you decide to major in international studies with the goal of working one day in Mexico or Central or South America. A minor in Spanish would be very helpful when you start looking for jobs!

WHAT DOES THE INSTITUTION DO FOR ISOCS?

In an effort to expand opportunities for students' success—and often as a result of activism on the part of ISOCs and their allies—postsecondary institutions are increasingly providing services specific to the unique needs of Indigenous Students and Students of Color.

Student Groups for Students of Color

Most postsecondary institutions will have student groups dedicated to various ethnic identities or cultural groups. Look to connect with these groups right away when you arrive on campus. These groups are a wonderful way to gain navigational capital: You will meet students from similar backgrounds, and many of these students, especially the club's officers (president, vice president, secretary, treasurer) will have been on campus for a few years and can answer questions and help you quickly navigate the campus as a new student. They are a wonderful source of guidance and advice on everything from which courses to take to which social activities are worthwhile.

At many universities these groups are called *unions*: the Native American Student Union, Black Student Union, Asian and Pacific Islander Student Union, for example. The student group for Latine students is usually known as MEChA (Moviemiento Estudiantil Chicanos de Atzlán), which is a national organization. These student groups can be a refuge and safe haven for you at the university. The authors were all members of such groups during their time at the university, and we stay in touch with the ethnic student groups at our universities. We often are advisors and mentors, we go to the meetings, get to know the students in the group, and advocate for them when necessary.

Multicultural Offices/Centers

Most every college and university has a multicultural office or center housed within the student services division that coordinates events and services for Students of Color. These offices or centers may have full-time university employees as well as student employees. The physical office or center space often becomes a hangout and gathering area for students. Be sure to visit the multicultural center on your campus and strike up conversations with the people (both employees and other students) you meet there.

Ethnic Studies Departments and Programs

Another important way to connect at your postsecondary institution, gain navigation capital, and even uncover or discover your own ethnic history and identity—especially if you come from a mixed family or have grown up away from your cultural home—is to take courses in ethnic studies.

Ethnic studies is a discipline that was born in the turbulent and revolutionary times of the 1960s civil rights struggles. Students of Color demanded universities teach texts, histories, and courses relevant to the lives of People of Color and no longer silence historically marginalized groups. They confronted administrators, professors, and even other students, often paying a steep price, and secured courses focused on the lives and histories of People of Color, as well as Faculty of Color to teach those courses.

Ethnic studies departments or programs offer a wide variety of classes, sometimes focused on single ethnic groups, and sometimes focused on multiple ethnic groups or themes and topics that have affected People of Color. Some universities have an ethnic studies department or program, other universities have departments devoted to single ethnic groups such as a Native American studies program or an African American studies department. Many of these programs and departments offer minors in ethnic studies or specific ethnic group studies. No matter what your major will be, you should consider doing a minor in ethnic studies.

Chief Diversity Officers and Offices of Diversity

Many colleges and universities now have an administrative position, usually at the VP level, dedicated to implementing and overseeing the university's diversity and inclusion efforts. In plain terms, chief diversity officers (CDOs) and offices of diversity are there to make sure Students of Color like you feel welcomed (safe and affirmed) at the university—as close to safe and affirmed as you would be among your community. These offices are there to minimize discrimination or barriers because of your race or other identity traits as you navigate through your time at your postsecondary institution.

Of course, you live in the real world and especially at a predominantly White institution (PWI) you know no one person or office can deliver such promises. Yet you should know that the CDOs and their offices are there for you. You should visit the office of diversity on your campus soon after you arrive.

Tribal Liaisons

Some postsecondary institutions may employ a tribal liaison who serves to help the university make connections among the tribal communities in the area or state in which the university is located. If you are an Indigenous student, be sure to see if your institution has a tribal liaison or tribal representative.

Some tribal liaisons also help professors interested in doing research among, and working in, tribal communities. Tribal liaisons are often both tribal members and alums of the university and are great resources for Native and Indigenous students, and indeed all Students of Color. Tribal liaisons can be incredibly helpful for Indigenous students who come from urban backgrounds or who have grown up away from ancestral/tribal communities. Tribal liaisons can help get you connected to the Indigenous community on campus and locally. You will realize you are not the only Indigenous student who has grown up away from their ancestral/tribal homeland.

Student Government

It is also worth noting that one excellent way for ISOCs to gain navigational capital in postsecondary education is to get involved with student government, as we described in Chapter 8. Many postsecondary institutions have a student government division where students can run for various offices across campus: student body president or vice president; student senators for colleges within the university; and many other student leadership positions within the university. Besides being a good place and time to hone your leadership skills, student government is a great way to influence university policies in ways that are sensitive to the student experience.

First-Year Experience Opportunities and Learning Communities for ISOCs

Many colleges and universities have opportunities specifically for first-year Students of Color, such as freshman interest groups (FIGs—more on this below) and extracurricular activities (and even housing). Some universities have *affinity housing* (on- or off-campus housing designed for identity-specific student groups), which can provide Students of Color with an immediate group of peers and older-student mentors. When you get to campus—and even before—you should ask the admissions office about these first-year opportunities.

Perhaps the most common first-year opportunity at the university is the FIG. FIGs bring together groups of students (called *cohorts*) who are interested in similar areas of interest, either personal or curricular, and have them register for the same cluster of classes. FIGs can help you navigate the university, create a class schedule and lock in **registration** (registration is the actual signing up for classes), and introduce you to students and professors who share your initial interests. FIGs also hold extracurricular events such as movie nights or study groups. You should definitely find out about FIGs before you arrive on campus.

> ***Think Alone/Think Together:*** What do you do when you have a conflict with someone of your own identity group? What if they are members of an ISOC student group that you love being a part of?

AS FORMER ISOCS, WHAT WE WISH WE HAD KNOWN WHEN WE STARTED COLLEGE

Who to Go to for Academic Support in a Class

You are not alone if you find yourself struggling in a class. We often struggled to succeed in our classes. Know that there are numerous places you can go for academic help and support. We suggest starting with your professor. We know this might be a frightening prospect. Professors can appear unapproachable at times, but we think you will often be surprised how approachable they can be. Professors have, in general, become professors in large part to help support you, and they want their students to be successful. Seeing their students succeed in class, continuing at the university, graduating, possibly going to graduate school, is something faculty enjoy and take pride in. Professors often help you understand what is important to know about what you are studying; they also help frame and explain assignments.

You could also seek help from the department's office staff. Depending on the department or program, office staff apply for positions where they can be on the front lines of support for students and help them be successful. You may be pleasantly surprised at the breadth of knowledge office staff have that will help you navigate the university experience.

The Importance of Going to Class

Postsecondary education is quite different from high school in that nobody—parents, siblings, relatives, school officials—will be continually checking to see if you are in class, or even if you are out of bed! It is tempting, after years of being in class, to simply skip class, blow it off, stay in bed, or do something you consider more enjoyable like playing video games or visiting with friends. But we strongly urge you to make going to class a top priority.

Perhaps more important, in-class activities (lectures, small-group work, videos, etc.) provide an opportunity to deepen what is most essential to focus on and learn in the class. Student questions, for example, often create new insights about key ideas. It is during class when professors will remind students of upcoming activities (exams, projects, written assignments), often providing more details about these requirements than is listed in the course syllabus. We cannot stress this enough: It is important that you attend every course. If you must miss class, be sure to notify the professor well ahead of time.

How to Navigate Campus

We wish that we had spent more time walking through all the buildings on campus and getting to know the offices. You can learn a lot by simply walking through a department, building, or office on campus. When you need to access a program or department, you will, as a result, know where to go. This is a simple and easy way to gain navigation capital.

How to Navigate Social Settings

We wish we knew better how to navigate social settings. Our presence on a university campus was the first time for most of us, as it may be for you, to be away from the comfortable familiarity of our communities and families. We were among the few Students of Color at PWIs. We found "our people," but we also had to interact with others (faculty and fellow students) who harbored various assumptions about us and our abilities given the stereotypes about our ethnic groups. What do you do when professors, students, or administrators make racist or stereotypical comments about you in social settings outside the classroom? (See Chapter 9 for strategies to deal with such situations.)

How to Advocate for Yourself

We wish we had known how to speak up for ourselves. We often found ourselves staying quiet in class or afraid to go to a professor's office, if we thought the professor had graded us incorrectly or *capriciously* (unpredictably; not according to the standards set out in the syllabus). We often did not know how to address some of the shortcomings we saw in our education, whether that was lack of courses related to our ethnic identities, or lack of student services for Students of Color. In short, we didn't know how to advocate for ourselves.

And here's the importance of advocating for yourself: In advocating for yourself, you advocate for those who will come after you. They may not have to encounter the same difficulties that you encounter. (See Chapter 7 for strategies to build your political and resistance capital to help you be in a better position to advocate for yourself.)

For some of the authors, the models for advocating for ourselves or speaking up for ourselves were more limited. We didn't have email or social media. Email has made contacting professors, staff, fellow students, and administrators very easy. However, with the ease of email come some potential pitfalls. We will explore some of those next.

COMMUNICATING WITH PROFESSORS

Email

Email has become the primary mode of official (and unofficial) communication within postsecondary education, especially between students and faculty. In fact, assume any email you send via the university email server can be made public. Traditional landline telephones are becoming obsolete at postsecondary institutions.

Email is usually the best way to get hold of faculty, but keep in mind each email to a faculty member (or university employee) has the potential to be misread or interpreted in ways you didn't intend. Each email also gives faculty a glimpse of your personality, or what a faculty member *might think* your personality is. It is safe to assume that professors, instructors, and lecturers (as well as staff) want a level of respect and formality from students, especially if they do not know students well or are meeting a student for the first time.

Email has become a form of social media in that there is nearly endless potential for the audience to interpret the message far differently than the author intended. So, a good rule of thumb is, *Be respectful and thoughtful when you email your professor.*

Let's assume, for example, that you are a first-year student about to begin your very first semester. You've enrolled in classes and want to see where your classrooms are before school starts so you are not wandering campus minutes before classes start looking for the right building and room number. You've visited all your classrooms except for English 101. You've checked the online class catalog at your university for the location of English 101, but you notice the classroom is "TBD" or *To Be Determined*. There's often a shortage of classrooms on campus so it's not unusual to have classrooms assigned at the last minute or even to have classroom locations switched during the first week of class.

In the online catalog you see the name Ruppert next to the English 101 course—you can assume that's the professor's last name—and an email. Of course, Professor Ruppert should know where their class is, and it's okay to email them to introduce yourself and ask questions. But keep your questions limited. You will receive a syllabus the first day of class—or perhaps earlier on the course website—and most of your questions will be answered in the syllabus.

Let's look at two hypothetical emails to Professor Ruppert and note the difference in tone:

Email 1

From: J Harris <email@universityemail.edu>
To: Professor Ruppert <email@universityemail.edu>
Subject: hey!!!!;)

> i think im in your class this semester lol so wheres class???? and what time???? also what books are there and do we have to read all them thx

---

Email 2

From: J Harris <email@universityemail.edu>
To: Professor Ruppert <email@universityemail.edu >
Subject: Question about the Location of English 101 this fall

> Dear Professor Ruppert,
> I hope you are well. My name is Jay Harris and I will be a student in your 9am English 101 course this coming fall semester. I looked at the course catalog online and noticed the location was TBD. I was wondering if you knew the location of the classroom. I'm a new student and am familiarizing myself

with campus and would like to visit all my classrooms before classes start. Thank you for your time and I look forward to meeting you.
Sincerely,
Jay Harris

The *tone* (tone is the author's attitude toward the subject matter and the emotional feeling of the writing) of the emails is vastly different and will be interpreted differently. Likely, the first email will be deleted or ignored. Professors receive dozens of emails a day and must prioritize which ones to respond to. The first email has annoyed Professor Ruppert right from the start with its subject line. The subject line is the first thing the professor sees in his inbox. Professor Ruppert may delete the email without even reading it due to the subject line alone. Professor Ruppert is not Jay Harris's buddy.

When reading the body of the first email, Professor Ruppert will note the informal, social media–like writing, the misspellings, the lack of a *salutation* (a *dear* or *hello* at the beginning of an email) and *closing* (the *thank you* or *sincerely* at the end of an email), the lack of a name, the misuse and overuse of punctuation, and will read the email in its entirety as lacking respect. Professor Ruppert may delete the email without responding knowing that the questions will be answered shortly: the location of the classroom will be made available in the course catalog as well as on the course website as soon as Professor Ruppert finalizes the syllabus. The question about whether a student must read all the texts for a class will strike Professor Ruppert as ridiculous.

After no response from Professor Ruppert to the first email, it is not unusual for students to send something like the following:

From: J Harris <email@universityemail.edu>
To: Professor Ruppert <email@universityemail.edu>
Subject: FW: hey!!!!;)
?????

From: J Harris <email@universityemail.edu>
To: Professor Ruppert <email@universityemail.edu>

Navigational Capital

Subject: hey!!!!;)
> i think im in your class this semester lol so wheres class???? and what time???? also what books are there and do we have to read all them thx

The student has ensured, with the resend of the email, that Professor Ruppert will begin English 101 annoyed. If Professor Ruppert does respond, it will no doubt be a short, angry email such as the following:

From: Professor Ruppert <email@universityemail.edu>
To: J Harris <email@universityemail.edu>
Subject: RE:FW:hey!!!!;)
> The syllabus with the location of the classroom is available on the course website.
> Dr. Ruppert

If a professor leaves off a salutation or closing, the hello and goodbye of an email, it is quite possible that they are annoyed. Professor Ruppert will come to the first English 101 pre-annoyed by Jay Harris, and Jay Harris will have to work to build mutual respect.

Sending an email to a professor is really about respect. Professors have spent long years in school becoming experts in their field. Treat the professor with respect.

Consider a potential reply from the professor to the second email. The second email had a clear subject line, a salutation, a clear message and question, and a closing. The professor felt the respect of the student and went out of their way to answer the question and connect with the student.

Reply from Professor Ruppert to Email 2

From: Professor Ruppert <email@universityemail.edu >
To: J Harris <email@universityemail.edu>

Subject: RE: Question about the Location of English 101 this fall

Dear Jay,

Nice to meet you (electronically) and thank you for your email. I think it's a great idea to locate your classrooms before classes start. My English 101 class will be in Russell Hall room 103. It's the big classroom to the right when you come in the front door. I'm happy to answer other questions you may have, and many of your questions might be answered on the syllabus which you can find online on the course website but do let me know if you have other questions. I look forward to meeting you in person.

Sincerely,

Dr. Ruppert

Professor Ruppert will come to the first English 101 class feeling a connection and mutual respect with the student.

To recap, here are our recommendations for email etiquette:

- Use the subject line and be clear about the subject.
- Address the professor as Dr. or Professor.
- Start with a quick pleasantry (*I hope you're doing well*).
- Be clear about what you are asking.
- End it with your name and "Thank you" or "Sincerely."

Most important: Keep in mind you should receive a syllabus the very first day of class. The answer to many of your questions is on the syllabus. The syllabus is a contract between the professor and student. You should read through the syllabus entirely and refer back to it often. You need not email the professor ahead of time with questions about how they are grading, how long the essays need to be, or when due dates are.

Think Alone/Think Together: The power of words: Words can make friends or enemies in an instant and create immediate conflict or

> harmony. Recall the term *language register*. It has to do with the words you choose. You probably use different language registers when you talk to teachers (formal) versus with your friends (casual). Why is your language different depending on whom you are talking to? What register might you use when communicating with fellow students? How will it be different when communicating with professors?

Visiting Office Hours

Every professor should have an office and every professor is expected—usually required by university policy—to hold weekly **office hours.** Office hours, simply put, are times a professor is expected to be in their office and available to students. Some professors prefer students to sign up for office hours, while others allow students to drop in unannounced. Some will conduct office hours virtually through Zoom or similar technology. The number of office hours expected from professors varies from institution to institution, but usually it will be 4–6 hours per week.

Remember the story that began this chapter? Teew got a cold reception from a professor. Perhaps it was because they didn't check when office hours were and just dropped by. Perhaps the professor was busy and slightly annoyed by the interruption. Perhaps the professor was intimidated—he's supposed to be the expert on Indigenous studies, but he couldn't speak a native language and he didn't want Teew's relatives undermining his authority. Or maybe the professor is simply a jerk.

You shouldn't hesitate to visit a professor's office during office hours. We recommend visiting all your professors during their office hours within the first 3 weeks of the semester. This is navigational capital in action. Have a specific purpose or question ready ahead of time before visiting your professor.

> **PRO TIP:** Make the most of office hours. These are specifically designed to assure students have access to their professors and instructors to seek guidance, gain clarification, and make meaningful connections.

Ask about a course assignment. If you cannot think of a question about class, ask the professor about their field of study. Tell them you find the class interesting and want to learn a bit more about how the professor became an expert in the field.

PRO TIP: Finally, make sure to connect with fellow students at the university or others in your program of study. Being just 1 or 2 years ahead of you in their journey they can be rich resources of information about how to apply and get into a specific program or college, which professors and classes are the most engaging and supportive within a program, and how to think strategically about your coursework, related internships, and career paths after you complete the degree.

OTHER IMPORTANT SOURCES OF NAVIGATIONAL CAPITAL

The Student Handbook

How do you know what the university expects of you as a student? A great resource for navigational capital is the student sandbook. It will detail all the policies your postsecondary institution has in place: what is expected of you in the classroom, in the dorm, and on campus. In the student handbook you will find policies on academic dishonesty (which is the university's term for cheating in class); where to find tech support (where you can get help with computer issues and advice on what software is free to you as a student); and what your costs will be (tuition and fees) and how to pay them. It provides a description of the colleges, departments, and major and minor course requirements Your college or university's student handbook is most likely online. It is a wealth of information and an important navigational asset.

The Course Catalog

All the courses offered by your postsecondary institution can be found online in the course catalog. In addition to descriptions of the courses, the catalog contains information and contact numbers for the departments and the names of faculty.

Student Health Services

Students can find doctors and nurses, counseling, therapy, addiction help, and even get prescriptions at the student health services office or center on campus. Some of the fees you pay as a student provide for these services, so do use them. You can learn about your institution's policies around alcohol and drugs on campus, which differ from local laws. The student health center will have information about local and campus sober-ride programs, which are often free. Many campuses do not allow alcohol on campus but do provide free rides to and from town or downtown for students who choose to go off campus to drink.

Work Study, Study Abroad, and Student Research

Postsecondary institutions have ways for you to make money as a student. When you get to campus, make sure to find out about **work study** programs. Work study is a federal program that provides funds for part-time employment to help with the cost of postsecondary education. You can often find work study jobs through your financial aid office on campus.

Also be sure to find the *study abroad* office on campus. Study abroad is the general term for course work students undertaken while living in a foreign country. In many colleges and universities, faculty regularly take their classes on trips to foreign countries. You can earn credit and experience the world through study abroad programs. Study abroad programs have financial help and are often looking for Students of Color.

Lastly, you may find *student research* opportunities working with professors and graduate students. Talk to the advisor in your major about the potential of working with professors on their research. Not only can such research opportunities expand and deepen your learning, they can also often help you get into graduate school if that is something you decide to pursue once you have your undergraduate degree.

We hope this chapter has been a useful guide to navigating the university. By simply reading through and understanding the information in this chapter,

> **PRO TIP:** Make some money and see the world during your time in postsecondary education. While there are off-campus work opportunities, on-campus work opportunities also provide financial support and sometimes can lead to additional opportunities available within the college or university.

you are enhancing and maximizing your navigational capital. Refer to this chapter often as you continue to acquire navigational capital throughout your first years at the university.

You got this. You can not only survive in college, university, or any postsecondary school you choose—you can thrive. In the words of the African American writer James Baldwin, "Those who say it can't be done are usually interrupted by others doing it" (Baldwin, 2012).

END OF CHAPTER ACTIVITY: REVERSE NAVIGATING YOUR DREAMS

We are often so caught up in the present, just getting through the small, everyday moments in our lives, that we don't often picture who and where we might be in 5, 10, or 20 years. In looking back over the years (decades) from when we, the authors, began our postsecondary educations, to where we are now in our careers, we realize that it took a lot of navigational capital to get us where we are. As importantly, we all navigated toward an image in our minds of who we wanted to be in the future.

In this end of the chapter activity, we'd like you to reverse-navigate where you'd like to be in 5, 10, or 20 years. What job do you see yourself in? What city or state or country do you live in? What does your neighborhood look like? Who are your people? What do you do for fun? Ask yourself these questions:

1. When you are at your happiest in life, what are you doing? Is there a job that relates to that happiness?
2. Who are your professional role models? Do you envision yourself as a lawyer arguing in front of a court? As an architect designing a

house or public building? As a scientist working at a university? A coach giving a halftime talk to a team? A psychologist working with people struggling to keep their lives together? A teacher working in a grade school? What do you picture yourself doing in 5 or 10 years? How does it relate to your happiness now, if it does?
3. Picture yourself walking into the first day of a new job a few months after college or university graduation. What is that job? What do you look like? What are you worried about? What are you excited about? Now picture yourself 10 years from now: You've overcome your anxiety and are considered an expert in your career. What do you look like? Where are you? Lastly, picture yourself 20 years from now: You're not only an expert, you have become a leader in your career. Maybe you have started your own business, maybe you have many employees working for you, maybe you are lecturing to young, eager students. What do you look like? Where are you?
4. So, how do you get from where you are now to that image of you in the future?
5. Use the navigational capital you've read about in this chapter and explore your postsecondary institution to point you toward answering that question. Start with the career services center, or the advising center, or even the admissions office. Tell them you have an image of yourself in the future and ask them, "How can you help me make that image a reality?"

NINE

Humanization Capital
Striving and Thriving

It is the beginning of the summer, and the five friends are back home after successfully making it through their first year of postsecondary education. They decide to meet at the same restaurant for burgers and fries to talk about how their first year of postsecondary school went, before they head to their summer jobs and other plans keep them busy.

> *Josephine:* Wow, I can't believe we've already made it through our first year of college. It flew by.
>
> *Teew:* Yeah, I know what you mean. There were a lot of days I wasn't sure I was going to make it. I wasn't sure I even wanted to go to college, then I had problems with that racist prof.
>
> *Anna:* What ever happened with that?
>
> *Teew:* I did what you suggested. I went to the Native Center and they hooked me up with a mentor. The prof who runs the center and the office associate were great. I ended up spending a lot of time there and it really helped. I even joined the Native Student group. I'm going to be in charge of throwing the parties next year.
>
> *Pancho:* I wish they had something like that at my school. People were nice enough, but there was almost no one that looked like me or spoke my language. Most of the social stuff they had I couldn't relate to. I felt pretty alone the whole first semester and kind of depressed. I even talked to someone in student affairs about leaving school. She gave me a flier for the counseling center. I went a couple of times. They had a circle group for minority students I started going to and I finally made some friends.

Josephine: My school is pretty diverse, but that doesn't mean everyone is nice. People say they care about diversity and stuff like that, but then people vandalized one of the pride flags that were put up for one of the celebrations, or there was this one guy in one of my classes who kept complaining about having to take an ethnic studies course for his degree.

Anna: I had a guy like that in my dorm. But he was even worse. He'd say racist things and then pretend he was joking and post offensive things on his room door. We complained and all they'd tell us is that he had "free speech rights." I quit walking by his door and I started going to the gym for yoga classes around the time he'd usually be in the commons area. Yoga helped a lot.

Kieran: The best thing I did all year was volunteering to help teach these local middle school kids basic web design as part of this coding club they set up. I went once in the fall as part of a service assignment for one of my classes and then stayed on. I'm going to help out next year too.

INTRODUCTION TO HUMANIZATION CAPITAL

In this chapter we explore the last of the forms of capital it will be important for you to develop and use as you successfully navigate your postsecondary educational journey: humanization capital. *Humanization capital* is "the process of becoming more fully human as social, historical, thinking, communicating, transformative, creative persons who participate in and with the world" (del Carmen Salazar, 2013, p. 126).

In the context of this discussion, humanization capital are the assets you bring and will rely on to withstand difficulties or recover from them when they occur—assets you will use to take full advantage of your educational experience and the many wonderful things it has to offer, while also maintaining your own humanness. These assets will allow you to hold on to and protect your sense of self, identity, and dignity in situations where that may not be easy. We believe that these assets will allow you to find joy and peace along your journey as well.

EXPLORING HUMANIZATION CAPITAL

One of the best things about postsecondary education is that it can provide a wealth of opportunities for you to grow and understand yourself as a human being and your place in the world. It can allow you to explore things you have never heard of before and develop gifts you never knew you had. However, one cannot pour from an empty cup. It is hard to thrive in your postsecondary education if most of your time and energy is spent simply trying to survive.

This is where humanization capital comes in. Developing and utilizing your humanization capital will help you fill up your spiritual and emotional cup and maintain your physical health. Focused on your well-being, humanization capital will help you build the skills and support you need to put you in a place where you can take full advantage of all that post-secondary education has to offer. Enacting our humanization capital, more broadly, seeks to assure that people see us, hear us, and value us as fully functioning human beings wherever we may find ourselves.

The transition from high school to postsecondary schooling, and the journey to successfully obtaining a degree, can be difficult for any student. For many, this will be the first time you may be away from family and friends and your primary support system for an extended period of time. It may be the first time in years you have had to make new friends. It may be the first time you have to make major decisions on your own, ones that can substantially affect your future. At the same time, you will likely have more freedom to do what you want, when you want, and how you want. But such increased freedom also comes with greater responsibility and accountability as you are treated as—and expected to behave as—an autonomous adult for the first time.

Consequently, mixed feelings of excitement, happiness, uncertainty, homesickness, and everything in between are common for students embarking on their postsecondary educational journey. Yet, students who come from nonmainstream communities, be they Communities of Color, less economically advantaged communities, LGBTQIA+, disabled, or similar communities, are likely to face challenges and situations that are not common for every student. This can be especially true for such students who find themselves at institutions with minimal diversity, or in states where local and state politicians may be working to undermine and attack important parts of their identities or the communities that they hold dear.

Unfortunately, each of the authors can recount times in our own postsecondary journeys where we experienced some form of dehumanization. Incredibly, some of these events occurred after we had obtained our advanced degrees and had secured our positions as university professors. Sadly, even your accomplishments will not shield you from the various forms of dehumanization that you might encounter. Yet, developing your humanization capital will help you build the tools and reserves necessary to not just withstand the difficult times, but to find ways to thrive and be successful as well.

As the vignette that opens this chapter highlights, there are a range of situations you might face if you enter postsecondary education as a member of one or more nonmainstream communities. Unfortunately, sometimes these situations involve attempts to dehumanize you, make you feel less than, and undermine your hopes and dreams. *Microaggressions*, as described earlier, are those often subtle and even sometimes unintentional "smaller" acts aimed at a person from a marginalized group on the part of fellow students, staff, faculty, the administration, or even outside community members, that can feel like repeated and hurtful jabs with a pin.

Outright racist, sexist, and homophobic conduct can be devastating, as can being singled out to represent one's community or having the value of your community ignored and discounted altogether. As the opening vignette illustrates, while the person in Anna's dorm may have had free speech rights, that does not erase or lessen the way in which such acts can feel like personal attacks or attempts to intimidate (as when just walking by the student's room and the common area made Anna feel uncomfortable).

As discussed more fully in Chapter 2, oppression as a strategy to dehumanize can be ideological, institutional, interpersonal, or internalized, or some combination of all four. Regardless of type, it can feel awful. Hopefully, during your time in postsecondary education you won't have to have any of these experiences. Thankfully, if you do, you have and can build on the assets necessary to not only survive but thrive during your time in college.

KEYS TO SURVIVING: USING AND BUILDING HUMANIZATION CAPITAL

First and foremost, even when you are not facing extreme stressors like some of those described in the above story, it is important to take care of yourself. It is hard to handle life in general, but especially when life is difficult, if you do not take care of yourself.

Eating well and getting enough sleep are often hard during college when preparing for exams sometimes leads to all-nighters and the late-night party can be hard to pass up. Yet, when you are physically run down and tired and not eating well, you are more prone to contracting illnesses, and mental and emotional challenges become that much harder. It can affect how you think and respond in certain situations. Accordingly, a crucial key to surviving and thriving in postsecondary education is to begin your journey with a plan to take care of your health (see the End of Chapter Activity).

One great thing about nearly every postsecondary institution is the services they offer to help students maintain their health and well-being. From student health and wellness centers, recreational activities and gyms, and mental health services, there are likely a range of options available to you to help you maintain your health, no matter where you might be attending school.

At the same time, homelessness and food insecurity are on the rise among college students. Most postsecondary institutions have created food pantries and partnered with local organizations to help students maintain the ability to have sufficient, healthy meals. Often the dean of students and housing offices can help with housing and shelter concerns. One part of the end-of-chapter exercise will help you identify and find the types of resources that may be of help or interest to you.

Please keep in mind that when we discuss health, we are referring to mental as well as physical health. As members of marginalized communities, we might be taught to minimize the harms that are done to us and to be tough and to not let such things bother us. Yet, the truth of the matter is that dealing with daily microaggressions and repeated acts of racism, bigotry, sexism, homophobia, and other kinds of harmful biases and aggressions takes its toll. That toll can become too difficult to bear when a person does not get help when it is needed. Seeking help is not a form of weakness. It is a sign of strength.

Just as one might engage in regular check-ups and wellness routines to maintain physical health, one can do the same to maintain one's mental health. Seeing a counselor regularly can be a good way to process through emotions, ideas, and situations before they become distressing and difficult. Participating in a support group, or engaging in meditation or relaxation activities, are examples of options as well.

Most postsecondary institutions provide counseling centers and other psychological health services, like wellness centers, that may include traditional counseling, but also opportunities to learn how to de-stress, cope, and relax. They also offer extensive gym and recreational opportunities, most of which will be included in your student fees or offered at low and affordable cost. Proactively taking care of yourself is not only a good use of your humanizing capital; it can also be a way to build your humanizing capital.

Finding a supportive community is important. As one colleague relayed to one of the authors:

> I unfortunately did not choose the most diverse or supportive college for People of Color. But I was fortunate enough to find a group of wonderful friends. They were always there when I needed to vent or process and we had a great time hanging out on nights and weekends. They made what would have been a mediocre experience at best, much better. In fact, years later they are still some of my best friends.

Having people you can be your authentic self with, who understand what you are going through, who listen supportively when you need to vent or rage, or who can give you good advice when you need it can help you manage even the toughest challenges you might face.

Keep in mind that supportive people and communities can sometimes come in forms and ways that you may not expect. Such people can be peers, but they can also be teachers, advisors, coaches, and staff members who might work in a range of capacities. They may even be people in the community outside of your postsecondary institution. Sometimes they may look like you and share other of your identity characteristics, and sometimes they may not. The important thing is that they see and value you as a full human being and recognize and support your worth.

YOUR HUMANIZATION CAPITAL: PITFALLS AND CAVEATS

It has been the authors' experience that not everyone who offers support, or who seems nice, actually is nice. Although most folks who may try to help you really are helpful, wonderful people, it is important to be aware of those who are more like wolves in sheeps' clothing. We call these false allies and supporters.

We have identified four types of people you are likely to encounter. First are those who are truly empowering and nurturing supporters. These are the people who get to know you and help you achieve your goals. In fact, they are often the folks who help you realize you can achieve and do more than you thought possible and are there to help and support you consistently along the way.

Second are those who do things that are supportive and may even be helpful, but they do not necessarily care about you or have your best interests at heart. For example, the faculty member that may give you a spot in their lab because their grant requires them to work on diversity. In these situations, the opportunity offered may still be a good one that you should take advantage of. But you should try to do so with your eyes open, recognizing that while helpful in some ways, in other situations that may not be the best person to go to when you need nurturing support.

The third are those who are ready with advice or who always seem to tell you the right things, but when push comes to shove their actions often do not match their words, or they do not actually act in a way that is supportive. For example, a person might tell you privately that they support the addition of LGBTQIA+ supportive services on campus, but then refuse to sign a petition asking for the same when asked.

Finally, there are those who may seem nice on the surface, but who are actually not supportive at all and may sometimes act in ways that are the opposite of support. For example, one of the authors had a school colleague whom she thought was a friend. This colleague was given information about an internship opportunity that she was told to disseminate to all members of the Black Student Alliance group. Rather than share the information as soon as it was provided, she waited until the application deadline had almost passed before sharing the information with her fellow students. She did this to make sure her own application arrived before the others and therefore

> **PRO TIP:** Trust your instincts and watch a person's actions. A person's actions will often tell you more about whether or not they are a true supporter than anything they might say.

received priority consideration, providing her an advantage. Those were not the actions of a supportive ally.

Unfortunately, it is not always easy to tell in which of the four categories a person might fall. However, one humanizing asset you have likely already developed as a person from a nonmainstream community is good instincts about people.

DON'T JUST SURVIVE, THRIVE

While much of this book has been focused on developing and using the assets that will allow you to successfully navigate the complexities and difficulties of postsecondary education, it is important to note that the whole reason we have written this book is to help you not just survive to graduation, but to offer tools so that you can thrive throughout your postsecondary educational journey and beyond.

While college certainly can be challenging and have speed bumps along the way, for many people their college years are also the most enjoyable, fulfilling, and positively life-changing years of their lives. This is especially true for those who can take full advantage of the college experience. Taking full advantage of the college experience will allow you to grow as a person, learn skills and develop abilities that will serve you well your whole life, make lifelong friendships, and have experiences you will treasure forever.

Finding Joy in Your Journey

One great thing about the college experience is it can be easily tailored to each individual. What follows are some suggestions for ways to make the experience enjoyable and fulfilling for you. We believe these are strategies that will allow you to build your humanizing capital and will help make college a great experience. While the following are a few suggestions, please note the main point is to become engaged and involved in the full college experience. While classes and studying are certainly important, they are only one piece of a full and fulfilling postsecondary education.

Find Your People

As noted above, finding a community can support and nurture you through the difficult times, and also help you find people with whom you can have fun. Join a club, play a sport, act in a play, take a class for fun, be part of an affinity group. In a word, follow your passions and interests wherever they might lead. All postsecondary schools have groups and activities you can join based on interest, identity, or both. Miss speaking Spanish with your abuela?—join the Spanish club. Always wanted to try pickle ball?—the class for beginners meets Tuesdays at 9:00. Love to build worlds in Minecraft?—those folks eat lunch together once a month.

The point is that you do and should bring your hobbies, interests, and passions with you to college. Finding others with common interests and passions can be a great way to enhance your overall experience and develop a supportive community. While college can certainly be a good place to build on existing interests and befriend others with whom you have a lot in common, it is also a wonderful place to meet all kinds of people and to have a range of new experiences and to learn and grow in many ways that will help you become a more fulfilled and self-actualized human being.

Postsecondary institutions regularly offer talks and lectures on all kinds of topics of interest. There are many entertainment opportunities offered at little or no cost. Concerts, plays, sporting events, festivals, college-wide traditional celebrations and activities, and other outings are just a few of the many options. As one of the authors notes:

> Coming from a small, rural town, I had never been to a Broadway play. During my first semester of college our dorm arranged a trip to see *Phantom of the Opera* at an old opera house in the city. I loved it, and have been a fan of musicals ever since.

In addition to entertainment opportunities, there will be opportunities for employment and internships (paid and unpaid), or to use class assignments to further your interests. Many majors offer the chance to earn credit for your work in an internship.

Internships are designed to give you "real world," hands-on experience in a particular area, and this can often open doors for permanent positions later on. For example, if you are an architecture major you might intern at a local design firm. You will be honing the skills you learned in class while working on projects for real clients, possibly resulting in an offer of permanent employment when you graduate if they like your work.

Similarly, many programs will offer "capstone" or "senior" projects, which are often independent projects designed to show your knowledge in a particular area. For example, if you are a dance major you might choreograph a piece to be performed in the end-of-year department show. However, even smaller class assignments can be opportunities to pursue an interest and deepen your learning.

Many professors will offer writing assignments that allow you to do research on a broad range of topics within the subject matter of a class. This can be a good time to explore further areas that may be of interest. Finally, even if your institution doesn't already have something available that is aligned with your interests, there are often opportunities and funding available to start something new. In fact, this is how many video gaming clubs and teams evolved on campuses across the country. As one student noted:

> When I first got to school there was no real community for LGBTQ students. I slipped a note into the suggestion box for our college dean, thinking it would go nowhere. Within a few months she helped me start an Advocates and Allies group. Within a year we went from having nothing to having one of the most vibrant and active groups within our college.

> **Think Alone/Think Together:** Make a list of 20 things that you enjoy or that bring you joy. What are some things you can do today, tomorrow, within a week or a few weeks to have fun and enjoy life? (note: can be small and inexpensive things).

At the end of the day, the whole point of postsecondary education is to enhance the quality of your life and to help you develop into the best version of yourself. Developing and utilizing your humanization capital will not only help you survive your college or university experience but will help you thrive and take full advantage of all postsecondary education has to offer.

Please keep in mind, though, that your time in postsecondary education is not an end in itself, but one step on what will hopefully be the long journey of your life. As educator, philosopher, and author Paulo Freire (2000) explains, "unfinishedness" and the practice of ever becoming our better selves is a natural part of being human. Developing your humanization capital is one important way to further develop your unfinished self.

As we close this chapter, and reflect on humanization capital, we'd like you to consider incorporating one additional concept as you move forward, that of gratitude. When things are difficult, taking a moment to reflect on what you may be grateful for can help you recognize and build on the good things in your life, even when those good things may be small or may be overwhelmed by all of the other things you are dealing with. Focusing on the good can help you maintain a positive outlook and keep you hopeful, two essential components of developing your humanizing capital and thriving during your time in postsecondary education.

While sharing gratitude with others, it's also important to give yourself grace and gratitude as part of self-care and being fully human. As Audre Lorde, author and activist, wrote in 1988, "Caring for myself is not self-indulgence, it is self-preservation, and that is an act of political warfare" (p. 131).

END OF CHAPTER ACTIVITY: CREATE YOUR PROACTIVE WELLNESS PLAN

As the old saying goes, "An ounce of prevention is worth a pound of cure." Taking that idea to heart, take a moment to think about ways that you decompress and deal with stress. Think about who you go to for comfort and support when things are difficult. Then think about what kinds of activities you would most like to be involved in—or try for the first time—when you are in college.

Then, make a list whether on an actual piece of paper or in an electronic document. On the left side, list three to five things you think you will need to feel happy, safe, and secure when you are at your postsecondary institution. On the right side list things you can do, or try, to make sure these needs are met. If you are not sure, try to think of where you can go for help in figuring that out.

Keep in mind, the purpose of this exercise is to get you thinking about what you might need before you need it. This list will inevitably and necessarily change as you gain experience and grow. You can come back to and repeat this exercise at any time, including when you do find yourself having difficulty and need to think through where you might find help.

Conclusion
Putting It All Together—Honoring Your Assets

You Made It! We hope that you have found helpful tips here for shaping your journey toward postsecondary education. Throughout the text, we have provided you with insights and tools to help you navigate the process of making decisions, from where to go to college all the way to how to thrive in the environment; how to embrace the surrounding community; your rights as a student; what you need to know about navigating the institution and getting the most out of the resources available; and above all encouraging you to enjoy your college experience. We hope you have taken advantage of the *Pro Tips, Think Alone/Think Together,* and *End of Chapter Activities* as you read through the text; if not, you can always go back and do them anytime. The whole point of this book is to help you be successful in your postsecondary journey.

"Success" will look different for everyone. There is no clear road map to "success" as defined in any book, but rather, it is the way you see the path forward leading to your goals, dreams, and aspirations. Pick up as many experiences as you can along the way. Get involved in campus activities, go to sporting events, explore buildings on campus you do not normally go into for classes, meet new people, and learn as much as you can about the world and, above all, about yourself.

Our purpose for writing this book was to share everything we, as ISOCs, wish we knew when we were students, or learned along our journeys. We encourage you, after reading the text, to take several concrete steps toward envisioning, imagining, and claiming your future. We hope you will take the tools offered in the text and learn and practice what makes sense to you to thrive and flourish in institutions of higher education and, in the process, find your most authentic self.

The assets you carry with you from your culture, community, family, and experiences in elementary and secondary education have given you the foundation you need to thrive. The values you have been raised with, and have gleaned from your culture, community, and family make you stronger as a person no matter where life takes you.

OUR PARTING WORDS

Throughout the process of writing this book, we kept coming back to the conversation about what we wish we had known back when we were thinking about going to college or in those first few years of postsecondary. We wanted to make the book accessible to our readers in a storied way. Following the experiences of five prospective students who go off to postsecondary education and reconnect at times to share their experiences gave us a way to add a narrative to the content of the book. **Anna, Josephine, Teew, Kieran,** and **Pancho** were created to help you experience the culturally empowered assets-based approach to postsecondary education for Indigenous Students and Students of Color with some immediacy. The vignettes we started each chapter with created a space for us to share part of our experience and those of the students we have mentored and supported as educators. We hope hearing and learning about these five students' thoughts, questions, and experiences made a difference in your understanding of the journey upon which you will embark.

Be proud of who you are and where you come from—carry that with you and you will thrive. Speak and live your truth in the world. And above all, embrace the joy in life.

An Open Letter to Faculty, Staff, and Advisors on Supporting Indigenous Students and Students of Color

Dear supporters of Indigenous Students and Students of Color,

Thank you for taking the initiative to acquire this book and educate yourselves on how best to support and serve our Indigenous Students and Students of Color preparing for or newly enrolled in postsecondary education institutions. The steps taken by Indigenous Students and Students of Color toward their future in the classroom and their chosen career are important strides not only for them but for their communities as well. They have stepped into a world where individuals like yourself can make or break their experience and their progress toward success.

    This letter shares our hopes and dreams for Indigenous Students and Students of Color and for all of you who support those students. You can help make the dreams of these students a reality.

    An assets-based perspective in postsecondary education is an essential approach to supporting the pursuit of degrees and future careers of Indigenous Students and Students of Color. We ask you to look for, identify, honor, and celebrate the assets of Indigenous Students and Students of Color as the starting point for providing advice and support. We ask you to recognize the potential of Indigenous Students and Students of Color who may have experienced academic challenges in the past. Attend to students' academic development as well as their social, emotional, college, and career development (Steen & Bethea, 2023) when attending to their navigational needs.

We ask you to reach out to Indigenous Students and Students of Color and practice mentoring from a relational and reciprocal frame evident in radical availability (Fulford, 2020). We need you, as much as possible, to be accessible to students who are searching for supports in higher education as they make their way through academia.

To best serve Indigenous Students and Students of Color we ask you to begin or continue on the journey toward your own self-reflection on racism, oppression, and bias. We are all biased, either unconsciously or consciously. We may find ourselves using our biases to project them onto others through microaggressions and prejudice. These microaggressions communicate verbal or nonverbal doubts toward the student and reflect a deficit perspective on their skills and ability to succeed. Resist the deficit model of education.

We ask you to counter microaggressions when they are used in your presence with or around students. We ask you to use micro-affirmations with Indigenous Students and Students of Color to instill confidence and project positivity toward them. And we ask you to practice micro-invitations with Indigenous Students and Students of Color to become involved in academic endeavors (research projects, TA, professional associations) available to them on campus. Keep them informed about academic and social opportunities.

Consider not only what it means to support, counsel, and advise but also to serve as an advocate and be an agent of change for Indigenous Students and Students of Color while they are in your care. You do this when you use your professional role on campus to push against policies, procedures, and practices that are oppressive to underserved students. We encourage you to take an anti-racist, pro-justice, and civil rights–driven stance in your work to support Indigenous Students and Students of Color by advocating for them with your colleagues and administrators.

Engage in the work to understand and practice what it means to be culturally competent, equity based, and culturally responsive in your actions (Ford et al., 2023). Language and actions matter in your role with Indigenous Students and Students of Color. Learn, appreciate, and advocate for cultural competency in your work to demonstrate to Indigenous Students and Students of Color that you are an ally to be trusted. Earning and protecting that trust will be essential to the success of the Indigenous Students and Students of Color you serve.

We encourage you to find those in your institution who are also practicing anti-racism, pro-justice, and civil rights beliefs and strategies while doing the necessary work to support Indigenous Students and Students of Color. Build a support team for yourself while you build a support team for the students. Do not be afraid to lean on those in your network; ask for help when you are faced with institutional resistance and policies and structures that seek to deny Indigenous Students and Students of Color their right to a culturally affirming, liberating education.

This book is focused on the ways Indigenous Students and Students of Color can be successful in preparing for and navigating through postsecondary education. We centered the conversation on how to embrace their cultural assets and be proud of who they have become. This text comes with navigational tools, applicable stories, tips to consider, and activities to engage them in thinking through decisions they may be faced with while in college.

For those students you are advising through the college application process we ask that you encourage students to use the personal essay in the application to focus on the ways their ethnicity and race have contributed to or defined their journey toward strength, courage, and resiliency. Encourage and support the students to embrace who they are, their identity as Indigenous Students or Students of Color, and how their culture has made them stronger. This essay affirms who each student is and how they were raised. Encouraging students to focus and celebrate themselves is an assets-based approach.

The path toward completion of a college degree can be daunting for any student, but Indigenous Students and Students of Color face a harder road. We ask you to read this book and practice an assets-based approach to empowering Indigenous Students and Students of Color so that they can reach the goals and dreams they have envisioned for themselves and their communities. Above all, reach out to the Indigenous Students and Students of Color you advise and support, being sure to check in with them throughout the semester. Make sure they know you are available and willing to assist them.

We have hope that you will take our words and turn them into actions with the Indigenous Students and Students of Color you work with now and in the future. Our hope is that you will empower and support Indigenous Students and Students of Color. We know and trust that you sincerely desire doing right by students who pass through your doors seeking to fulfill a dream and living out the aspirations of their ancestors. Practicing a culturally empowered, assets-based approach to supporting Indigenous Students and Students of Color will lead you to the path of being a change agent.

Thank you for your commitment to the success of Indigenous Students and Students of Color!

Glossary of Terms

ancestral capital: the roots of one's ancestral legacy, one's ancestral funds of knowledge, talents, and ways of being that come from one's ancestors especially before colonization.

aspirational capital: the ability to maintain hopes and dreams for the future even in the face of real or perceived barriers.

asset: a useful or valuable thing, person, or quality. Typically, we think of human assets, institutional assets, physical assets, and cultural assets.

assets-based view: a view that focuses on one's strengths and abilities including how to further develop them and use them to advantage.

Asian American and Pacific Islander: refers to all people who have roots and ancestry in Asia and the Pacific Islands.

assimilation: the process of forcing, coercing, encouraging, or demanding that students and their families conform to the dominant mainstream culture (cultural assimilation), while also eliminating any language or dialect outside of what is considered standard English (linguistic assimilation).

Black: refers to all people who have African roots and ancestry including those who define themselves as African American.

campus: the setting (physical place) of the postsecondary institution.

career services office: office, center, area, or group of people on campus whose job it is to connect students with job opportunities and to work with students to develop their professional portfolio of documents and skills (resume, writing sample, interviewing skills, etc.) in order to aid in obtaining a job.

cis-gendered: a person whose gender identity is consistent with their sexual identity at birth.

community cultural wealth: the accumulation of all forms and kinds of cultural capital held by a particular social and cultural identity group to survive and resist racism and the various forms of oppression. These forms of capital serve as strengths and resources to Communities of Color.

cultural assets: cultural assets such as the arts, music, language, traditions, stories, and histories that make up a community's identity, character, and customs.

cultural capital: those things valued by a group or community that contribute to the identity and unity of that group or community. It includes the specific forms of knowledge, skills, and abilities that are valued by a particular group.

cultural community: a group of people who share some common traditions that continually change both the individual and the community.

deficit-based view: a view that focuses on what a person does not know, and on what skills and experiences they do not have.

diaspora: the movement of people from their traditional homelands; for example, the relocation of Mexican people to the United States is considered the Latino diaspora.

discrimination: acting on one's prejudices. Such actions may be overt and explicit, such as threats, slander, and ridicule, or covert and implicit, such as ignoring or avoiding others because of prejudices.

discursive capital: the actual doing of community cultural wealth in ways where you share and apply your cultural knowledge and the specific skills of well-being in ways that foster action.

ecological capital: the relational knowledge about nature, the environment, and all ecology wherein people connect to and see themselves interdependent on the land and the environment.

extracurricular activities: those pursued beyond normal course work and activities assigned in classrooms.

Glossary of Terms

familial capital: the cultural knowledge nurtured among *familia* (kin) that carries a sense of community history, memory, and cultural intuition.

general education requirements or ***Gen Eds.:*** a group of classes that all students of the college or university are required to take, usually in their first 2 years, to help students achieve a well-rounded education in multiple areas. General education requirements are the key to a liberal arts education.

higher education: any education received after graduating from high school. Often used interchangeably with the term "postsecondary education."

humanizing capital: the process of becoming more fully human as social, historical, thinking, communicating, transformative, creative persons who participate in and with the world.

ideological oppression: the idea that one group of people, based on any number of demographic differences, is better than another and therefore has a right to dominate the other group.

Indigenous: refers to those who have roots and ancestry in the First Peoples or First Nations of a given geographical area.

Indigenous Students and Students of Color (ISOC): refers to students from communities and cultures that have historically and contemporarily been marginalized and/or oppressed due to systemic, political, and cultural structures. This includes all parts of a person's intersectional identity, including but not limited to race, ethnicity, national origin, religion, gender identity, sexual orientation, class, and any other salient characteristic that enables a person to define who they are.

individual identity: personal characteristics an individual has attachment to and regards with respect to "who they are."

institutional oppression: the idea—based on ideological oppression—that control of one group over another is justified. This control occurs in the policies, procedures, and practices of major institutions such as the legal system, the banking system, the political system, and the education system.

internalized oppression: the idea that some members of subordinated groups come to believe the ideas about them and their group (ideological oppression), experience their lack of access and decision-making in schools, courts, banks (institutional oppression), and have day-to-day encounters of disrespect and dehumanization (interpersonal oppression).

internships: professional opportunities to experience an area of interest (such as a career or job) that offers meaningful, practical work.

interpersonal oppression: the idea that one person or group of people has the right to dehumanize, in many ways, another person or another group of people.

intersectionality: the focus on multiple identities and their relationship to power.

Latine: refers to all people of Latin American and Caribbean roots and ancestry who may define themselves as Latina, Latino, or Latinx.

linguicism: the ideologies, structures, and practices that create unequal differences in power and access to resources based on language.

linguistic capital: the intellectual and social skills learned through communication experiences in more than one language or style.

lower-division courses: classes offered at the freshman (often these course numbers begin with 100 or 1000) and sophomore (200 or 2000) levels.

major: an area of intensive study often completed during the last 2 years of college.

microaggressions: often subtle and sometimes even unintentional "smaller" acts aimed at a person of a marginalized group as a result of prejudice or as a way to devalue, discount, or undermine.

navigational capital: the skills of maneuvering through social institutions (such as banks, businesses, government agencies, etc.) so that one's needs can be addressed and met.

office hours: times a professor is expected to be in their office and available to students.

oppression: the systemic injustice or cruel exercise of authority or power by dominant groups against those who are subordinate.

political capital: the assets an individual or group possess that allows them to influence the structures, institutions, or situations around them in a way that is positive and advantageous for themselves, or for others on whose behalf they might advocate.

postsecondary education: any education received after graduating from high school. Often used interchangeably with the term "Higher Education."

praxis: reflecting upon and acting to transform oppressive systems; this leads to further reflection and so on.

prejudice: learned prejudgments including internal thoughts, feelings, attitudes, and assumptions about people from different social groups based on stereotypes.

racism: cultural prejudice and discrimination, supported intentionally or unintentionally by institutional power and authority, used to the advantage of Whites and the disadvantage of People of Color.

registration: the signing up for classes.

resistance capital: knowledges and skills fostered through oppositional behavior that challenge inequality and strive for social justice.

social capital: the networks of people and community resources one relies upon, including adults and teachers.

social identities: characteristics of the self influenced by and connected to groups to which one has an affinity.

sociocultural Identity: characteristics of the self influenced by and connected specifically to one's cultural orientation that are shared by others.

spiritual capital: the sense of hope and faith, rooted in a connection to a reality greater than oneself.

stereotypes: reduced or simplified characteristics attributed to a group of people based on race, ethnicity, language, religion, sexual identity, sexual orientation, and other elements of identity.

Students of Color: refers to students who self-identify as persons with membership in an ethnic, cultural, and/or racialized and minoritized group.

targeted universalism: the goal to give everyone the opportunity to be successful while recognizing that different strategies will be required for different sociocultural identity groups.

tenure: a status received by an instructor at a college or university after a trial period that carries protections against unjust dismissal.

theory: a "set of knowledges" that describes how we think something works.

upper-division courses: classes at the junior (often these courses begin with 300 or 3000) and senior (400 or 4000) levels.

work study: a federally funded program that enables enrolled students to work various jobs across campus through money provided by the federal government.

References

Anzaldúa, G. (1990). Haciendo caras, una entrada. In G. Anzaldúa (Ed.), *Making face, making soul: Creative and critical perspectives by feminists of color* (pp. xv-xxviii). Aunt Lute Books.

Anzaldúa, G. (1999). *Borderlands/La Frontera: The new Mestiza* (2nd ed.). Aunt Lute Books.

Baldock, P. (2010). *Understanding cultural diversity in the early years*. SAGE Publications Ltd. Available at: https://doi.org/10.4135/9781446288108

Baldwin, J. (2012). *Notes of a native son*. Beacon Press.

Bell, J. (2013). *The four "I's" of oppression*. YouthBuild USA.

Benavides, C. (2017, October 16). Students walk out after teacher orders: Speak" "American." *NBC News*. https://www.nbcnews.com/news/latino/students-walk-out-after-teacher-tells-students-speak-american-n811256

Chavez, C. (1984, November 9). *Speech to the Commonwealth Club of California*. https://libraries.ucsd.edu/farmworkermovement/essays/essays/CESAR%20CHAVEZ%20COMMONWEALTH%20SPEECH.pdf

Cuauhtin, R. T. (2019a). We have community cultural wealth!: Scaffolding Tara Yosso's theory for classroom praxis. In R. T. Cuauhtin, M. Zavala, C. Sleeter, & W. Au (Eds.), *Rethinking ethnic studies* (pp. 244–280). Rethinking Schools.

Cuauhtin, R. T. (2019b). The four "I's" of oppression. In R. T. Cuauhtin, M. Zavala, C. Sleeter, & W. Au (Eds.), *Rethinking ethnic studies* (pp. 216–219). Rethinking Schools.

del Carmen Salazar, M. (2013). A humanizing pedagogy: Reinventing the principles and practice of education as a journey toward liberation. *Review of Research in Education, 37*(1), 121–148.

Delpit, L. (2014). Multiplication is for White people. In W. Au (Ed.), *Rethinking multicultural education* (pp. 17–24). Rethinking Schools.

Diaz-Rico, L. (2017). *The crosscultural, language, and academic development handbook*. Pearson.

Ford, D. Y., Moore, J. L., & Peebles, E. (2023). A perfect storm: Educational factors that contribute to miseducation and underachievement among Black students. In *Black Males in secondary and postsecondary education* (Vol. 9, pp. 45–66). Emerald Publishing Limited.

Franquiz, M., & Salazar, M. (2004). The trans-formative potential of humanizing pedagogy. *High School Journal, 87*(4), 36–53.

Freire, P. (1970). *Pedagogy of the oppressed*. Continuum.

Freire, P. (2000). *Pedagogy of freedom: Ethics, democracy, and civic courage*. Rowman & Littlefield Publishers.

Fulford, A. (2020). Re-thinking the mentoring relationship: Gabriel Marcel, availability and unavailability. In C. Woolhouse, & L. J. Nicholson (Eds.), *Mentoring in higher education* (pp. 155–173). Springer.

Galván, R. (2006). Campesina epistemologies and pedagogies of the spirit: Examining women's sobrevivencia. In D. Delgado Bernal, C. A. Elenes, F. E. Godinez, & S. Villenas (Eds.), *Chicana/Latina education in everyday life: Feminista perspectives on pedagogy and epistemology* (pp. 161–179). SUNY Press.

Goodman, S. (2023, January 23). Native languages are disappearing. Colleges could help preserve them. *The Chronicle of Higher Education*. https://www.chronicle.com/article/native-american-languages-are-disappearing-colleges-could-help- preservethem#:~:text=According%20to%20the%20Administration%20for,a%20few%20fluent%20speakers%20remaining

Grande, S. (2004). *Red pedagogy: Native American social and political thought*. Rowman & Littlefield Publishers.

GroundWork USA (n.d.). *What is an asset?: Examples and definitions*. https://groundworkusa.org/eqdevtools/asset-examples/

Group Health Foundation (2023, January). *The living language guide*. Author. https://inatai.org/wp-content/uploads/2022/09/Living-Language-Guide-jan2023.pdf

Gutiérrez, K., & Rogoff, B. (2003). Cultural ways of learning: Individual traits or repertoires of practice. *Educational Research, 32*(5), 19–25.

Hall, E. (1976). *Beyond culture*. Anchor Books.

Hanh, T. N. (2007). *The art of power*. HarperOne.

Hardy, A. (2022, February 14). The wage gap between college and high school grads just hit a record high. *Money*. https://money.com/wage-gap-college-high-school-grads/

Harjo, J. (2013). *Crazy brave: A memoir*. W. W. Norton & Company.

References

Jung, C. G. (1981). *The archetypes and the collective unconscious* (Bollingen Series XX). Princeton University Press.

Kendi, I. X. (2019). *How to be an antiracist.* One World/Ballantine.

Khan, S. (2021, April 27). 3 reasons post-secondary education is so crucial today. *EEqual.* https://eequal.org/3-reasons-post-secondary-education-is-so-crucial-today/

King, M. L. (1963, April 16). *Letter from Birmingham jail.* Reprinted and available at: https://www.csuchico.edu/iege/_assets/documents/susi-letter-from-birmingham-jail.pdf

King, M. L. (1968, March 14). *The other America.* https://www.gphistorical.org/mlk/mlkspeech/

Kohl, H. (1994). *I won't learn from you.* New Press.

Lorde, A. (1988). *A burst of light.* Firebrand Books.

Moll, L. C., Amanti, C., Neff, D., & Gonzalez, N. (1992). Funds of knowledge for teaching: using a qualitative approach to connect homes and classrooms, *Theory into Practice, 31*(2), 132–141.

Nevárez, D. M. (2022). Toward recognizing and leveraging Latinx teacher candidates' community cultural wealth. In C. Gist and T. Bristol (Eds.), *Handbook of research on teachers of color and indigenous teachers* (pp. 265–282.) American Educational Research Association.

Obama, B. (2008, February 5). Barack Obama's Feb. 5 Speech. *New York Times.* https://www.nytimes.com/2008/02/05/us/politics/05text-obama.html

Office of Faculty Development, California State University, Chico (n.d.). *Linguistic capital.* https://www.csuchico.edu/fdev/fdev-teaching-guides/teachingguide-36.shtml

Oxford English Dictionary (n.d.). *Dialect.* https://www.google.com/search?q=dialects&oq=dialects&aqs=chrome..69i57j0i20i263i512j0i512l5j0i20i263i512j0i512l2.2541j1j7&sourceid=chrome&ie=UTF-8

powell, j., Menendian, S., & Ake, W. (2019). *Targeted universalism: Policy & practice.* Othering & Belonging Institute, University of California, Berkeley. https://belonging.berkeley.edu/targeted-universalism

Pratt, R. H. (1892). The advantages of mingling Indians with Whites. In I. C. Barrows (Ed.), *Proceedings of the National Conference on Charities and Correction, 19th annual session* (pp. 45–59). Press of Geo. H. Ellis.

Rosales, J., & Walker, T. (2021, March 30). The racist beginnings of standardized testing. *National Education Association.* https://www.nea.org/nea-today/all-news-articles/racist-beginnings-standardized-testing

Sensoy, O., & DiAngelo, R. (2017). *Is everyone really equal?: An introduction to key concepts in social justice education*. Teachers College Press.

Skibba, R. (2018, November). How a second language can boost the brain. *Knowable Magazine*. https://knowablemagazine.org/article/mind/2018/how-second-language-can-boost-brain?gclid=CjwKCAjw-KipBhBtEiwAWjgwrCfPosnAUY1Y3dR0dQWTssaBfAqdHau1O47XixBuT1xYG9IvMPVHQhoC2yoQAvD_BwE

Skutnabb-Kangas, T. (2015). Linguicism. *The encyclopedia of applied linguistics*. Blackwell. https://doi.org/10.1002/9781405198431.wbeal1460. http://www.tove-skutnabb-kangas.org/dl/310-Skutnabb-Kangas-Tove-2015-Linguicism-Encyclopedia-of-Applied-Linguistics-Blackwell.pdf

Sleeter, C. (2020, June). Critical family history: An introduction. *Genealogy*, 4(2),64. https://www.christinesleeter.org/critical-family-history

Solórzano, D. G., & Delgado Bernal, D. (2001). Examining transformational resistance through a critical race and LatCrit theory framework: Chicana and Chicano students in an urban context. *Urban Education*, 36(3), 308–342.

Steen, S., & Bethea, C. (2023). Exploring group counseling interventions for Black boys in middle school: Using the Achieving Success Everyday (ASE) Group Model for Racial and Mathematical Identity Development. In *Black males in secondary and postsecondary education: Teaching, mentoring, advising and counseling* (pp. 67–85). Emerald Publishing Limited.

Stern, J. (January 2022). *Cultural asset mapping project, City of Austin; PlannersWeb.com, Metropolitan Area Planning Council's Arts & Culture Department*. https://blog.americansforthearts.org/2022/01/20/cultural-asset-identification-building-inclusive-creative-economies

Szasz T. (1973). *The second sin*. Anchor Press.

United Farm Workers (n.d.). *Education of the heart: Cesar Chavez in his own words*. https://ufw.org/research/history/education-heart-cesar-chavez-words/

United States Census Bureau (2021, April 21). *Educational attainment in the United States:2020*. https://www.census.gov/data/tables/2020/demo/educational-attainment/cps-detailed-tables.html

Yosso, T. (2005). Whose culture has capital? A critical race theory discussion of community cultural wealth. *Race Ethnicity and Education*, 8(1), 69–91.

Yosso, T. J., & Garcia, D. G. (2007). "This is no slum": A critical race theory analysis of CCW in Culture Clash's *Chavez Ravine*. *Aztlan: A Journal of Chicano Studies*, 32(1), 145–179.

Yosso, T. J. (2013). *Critical race counterstories along the Chicana/Chicano educational pipeline*. Routledge.

Index

The letter *f* after a page number indicates a figure.

2-year postsecondary institutions, 46
4-year postsecondary institutions, 47

AAVE (African American Vernacular English), 95
Abuse, 119–121
Academic achievement, 36–37
Academic language, 97
Academic majors and minors, 39, 44–45, 80–81, 150–152, 151–152
Access, 1
ACT (test), 53
Activism, 128–129
Administration organizational chart, 145f
Admissions criteria, 51
Advising, 147–148
Advocacy. *See* Student advocacy
Advocacy for students. *See* Role models/mentors
Advocates for students. *See* Role models/mentors
Affinity housing, 155
Affirmative action, 2
African/African American studies, 37
Agency, 130–132
Ake, W., 10
Amanti, C., 23
Ancestral capital. *See* Cultural (and ancestral) capital
Anzaldúa, G., 19, 21, 104

Application essay, 53–54, 59
Applying to a postsecondary institution, 38–39, 51–55
Aspirational capital
  activity, 59
  college and career planning, 44–51
  college application and admissions, 51–55
  financial planning, 55–58
  introduction and overview, 25, 28, 33–35, 58–59
  vignette, 32–33
Assets, 13–16, 17. *See also* Capital types by name
Assets-based approach, 15–16, 21
Authors' aspirational narratives
  Bridgeman, J., 35–38
  Jaime, A., 38–39
  Rios, F., 39–40
  Roxas, K., 40–42
  Russell, C., 42–44
Awareness raising, 131

Baldock, P., 65
Baldwin, J., 166
Barriers to success, 33, 34
Bell, J., 75
Benavides, C., 99
Benefits of postsecondary education, 3–4
Bethea, C., 184
Bilingual education, 98–99

Bilingualism, 95
Black English, 95
Black Lives Matter movement, 1
Board of trustees, 144
Bridgeman, Jacquelyn, 35–38

Campus, 12, 157
Capstone projects, 177
Career advising, 44–45
Career choice, 44–45
Chapter overviews, 27–31
Chavel, C., 139
Chicano/Latino, 39–40
Civil rights law, 135–136, 139
Civil Rights Movement, 1
Class academic support, 156
Class assignments, 81–82
Class attendance, 156–157
Collective resistance, 137–138
College and career planning, 44–51
College application and admissions, 51–55
College definition, 47
College majors and minors. *See* Academic majors and minors
Colonization, 129–130
Communication skills, 137
Communication style, 93
Communities of Color, 4
Community, 40–42, 176–177
Community assets, 15–16, 17–18
Community-based organizations, 84
Community colleges, 46
Community cultural wealth, 12, 27–28
Contextual identity, 67
Course academic support, 156
Course catalog, 164
Crazy Brave (Harjo), 31
Credit card scams, 57–58
Cuauhtin, R. T., 25–26, 28, 30, 63, 75, 91, 132
Cultural capital. *See* Cultural (and ancestral) capital

Cultural (and ancestral) capital. *See also* Community cultural wealth
activity, 86–87
and assets-based approach, 22–24
and culture, 64–66
identifying assets, 72–73, 86–87
and personal identity, 61–62
sociocultural identity, 63–64, 85–86
strengthening assets, 79–85
and terminology, 12
Culture, 64–66, 68

Deans, 144
Deficit-based view, 16, 17–18, 21
Deficit orientation, 21
Dehumanization, 171
Del Carmen Salazar, M., 26, 30, 169
Delgado Bernal, D., 23, 133
Delpit, L., 24
Department chairs, 146–147
DiAngelo, R., 65, 74
Diaz-Rico, L., 93
Direct admissions, 50–52
Discursive capital, 26
Diversity efforts, 2, 154
Documents, 55
Dominant narrative, 17–18
Dreaming, 33–34
Due process, 136

Ebonics, 95
Ecological capital, 26
Educational attainment, 5–6, 35–36
Emailing a professor, 158–163
Empowerment, 129
Essentializing culture/race/ethnicity, 68
Ethnicity, 43, 47, 66–67, 68, 81, 153
Ethnicity-specific colleges, 47
Ethnic studies, 39, 81, 153
Eurocentrism, 71
Exclusion, 90–91
Extracurricular activities, 83–84

Index

Faculty, 147
FAFSA (free application for federal student aid), 56–57
Familial and social capital
  activity, 125–127
  case studies, 117–121
  overview, 107–113, 124–125
  and postsecondary setting, 113–116
  and roadblocks in postsecondary education, 116–121
  strengthening assets, 121–127
  vignette, 105–107
Familial responsibilities, 117–119
FIGs (freshmen interest groups), 155
Filipino community, 40–42
Financial assistance, 56–57
Financial planning, 55–58
Fiscal responsibility, 58
Fluid identity, 67
Ford, D. Y., 185
Formatting used in this work, 7
Franzuiz, M., 111
Free Application for Federal Student Aid (FAFSA), 56–57
Freire, P., 76, 133, 178
Freshmen interest groups (FIGs), 155
Fulford, A., 184

Galván, R., 26
Garcia, D. G., 1, 24
General education requirements, 149–150
Gonzalez, N., 23
Goodman, S., 90
GPA (grade point average), 52
Grade point average (GPA), 52
Graduate students, 147
Graduation requirements, 148–149
Grande, S., 10
Gratitude, 178
Groundwork USA, 12, 13
Group Health Foundation, 9n2
Gutiérrez, K., 68

Hardy, A., 129
Harjo, J., 30
HBCUs (historically Black colleges and universities), 47
Health, 138, 172–173
Heritage language, 101–102
Higher education. *See* Postsecondary education
Hispanic-serving institutions (HSIs), 48
Historically Black colleges and universities (HBCUs), 47
HSIs (Hispanic-serving institutions), 48
Humanization capital
  activity, 178–179
  background, 169–173
  definition, 26
  pitfalls and caveats, 174–175
  types of people, 174–175

Iceberg model of culture, 66f
Immigrant experience, 41–42, 43
Inclusion, 89–90
Indigenous languages, 99–101
Indigenous peoples and culture, 4, 11–12, 38, 42–43, 48, 154
Indigenous students and Students of Color (ISOC), 11–12
Indigenous studies, 39
Individual assets, 15–16, 17
Individual path, 180
Inequities in postsecondary education, 2
Institutional cultures, 65
Institutional funding, 47
Institution choice, 48–51
Institution types, 45–48
Interactive features of this work, 7–8
Interests. *See* Personal interests
Internet research, 48–49
Internships, 45, 177
Interpersonal language, 97
Intersectionality, 69–70
ISOC (Indigenous students and Students of Color), 11–12

Jaime, Angela M., 38–39
Jung, C. G., 72
Junior colleges, 46

Kendi, I. X., 74
Khan, S., 3
Kindness as act of resistance, 133–134
King, M. L., 1, 125
Knowledge as power, 135–136, 139
Kohl, H., 73

Language education, 102–103
Language register, 93
Languages, 37, 41–42, 88–89, 93–94, 99–101, 101–102. *See also* Linguistic capital
Latino/Chicano, 40–41
Letters of recommendation, 51–52
Liberation, 129
Lifestyle, 172
Linguistic capital
 activity, 104
 expanding your assets, 94–96
 identifying your assets, 17, 96–97
 introduction to, 89–95
 linguicism, 97–98
 strengthening language skills, 101–104
 vignette, 88–89
Living at home, 49–50
Lorde, A., 178

Major. *See* Academic majors and minors
Menendian, S., 10
Mental and physical health, 138, 172–173
Mentors/role models. *See* Role models/mentors
Microaggressions, 134, 171
Minority status, 36–37, 41
Mixed ethnicity, 43
Moll, L. C., 23
Moore, J. L., 185

Multicultural centers, 153
Multiple identities, 67, 69–70

Native Americans. *See* Indigenous languages; Indigenous peoples and culture; Indigenous students and Students of Color (ISOC)
Navigational capital
 activity, 166–167
 background, 141–142
 communicating via email, 158–163
 miscellaneous information, 156–158
 office hours, 163–164
 personnel, 144–148
 program requirements, 148–152
 support services, 152–156
 and this work, 27
Neff, D., 23
Negativity, 73–74
Nevárez, D. M., 91
Nonparticipation as resistance, 132–134

Obama, Barack, 59
Office hours, 163–164
Office of Faculty Development, 93
Oppression, 69, 75–79, 97–101, 129–130
Oxford English Dictionary, 93

Passions, 81, 176
Patriarchy, 71
Peebles, E., 185
Personal growth, 3–4
Personal interests, 81, 176
Physical and mental health, 138, 165, 172–173
Pit River Tribe, 38
Political and resistance capital
 activity, 139–140
 background, 25, 130–134
 and education system, 129–130
 pitfalls and caveats, 134
 vignette, 128–129
Political context, 1–2

Index

Post-COVID period, 1
Postsecondary education
  access, 1
  benefits of, 3–4
  choosing an institution, 48–52
  inequities, 2
  preparation for, 58–59
  success in, 5, 174–175
  terminology, 12
  types of institutions, 45–48
Powell, j., 10
Power relationships, 64
Pragmatics, 92
Pratt, R. H., 100
Praxis, 134
President and vice presidents, 144, 146
Professional degrees, 47
Provost, 144
PSAT (test), 53

Quality of life, 4

Race, 66–67, 68
Racism, 37, 74–75
Reflections, 134
Representing your social-identity group, 82
Resistance capital, 25. *See also* Political and resistance capital
Rios, Francisco, 39–40
Rogoff, B., 68
Role models/mentors, 37, 39, 40, 82–83
Rosales, J., 52
Roxas, Kevin, 40–42
Russell, Caskey, 42–44

Salazar, M., 111
SAT (test), 53
Scholarships, 52–53
School-choice considerations, 48–51
School climate, 128
Self-actualization, 129
Self-advocacy, 157–158

Semantic differences in language, 91–92
Senior projects, 177
Sensoy, O., 65, 74
Skibba, R., 95
Skutnabb-Kangas, T., 97
Sleeter, C., 87
Social assets. *See* Familial and social capital
Social capital. *See* Familial and social capital
Social settings, 157
Sociocultural identity, 63–64, 85–86
Solórzano, D. G., 23, 133
Spiritual capital, 26
Staff, 147
Standard dialects, 94
Standardized tests, 51, 52–53
Status, 92–93
Steen, S., 184
Stereotypes, 74–75
Stern, J., 26, 63
Strategic identity, 67
Student advocacy, 130–132
Student clubs, 83
Student expectations, 36–37, 38, 40
Student government, 154–155
Student groups, 152–153
Student handbook, 164
Student health center, 165
Student housing, 50–51, 155
Student loans, 57
Student research, 165, 177
Student support services, 84–85
Student unions, 152–153
Study-abroad programs, 165
Support networks, 122–123
Syntactic differences in languages, 92
Szasz, T., 64

Tagalog, 41–42
Technical schools, 45–46
Terminology used in this work, 7, 11–13
Test bias, 52
Theory and academic vocabulary, 19–21

Thich Nhat Hanh, 85
This work. *See also* Authors by name
   formatting, 7
   interactive features, 7–8
   and navigational capital, 27
   overview of chapters, 27–31
   terminology, 7, 9–13
Tlingit identity, 43
Tribal liaisons, 154
Tribally controlled colleges and universities, 48
Tuition, 50
Types of postsecondary institutions, 45–48

Uncertainty, 34–35
"Unfinishedness," 178
United Farm Workers, 139
Universities and colleges, 46–48
U.S. Census Bureau, 5f

Volunteering, 45, 85, 131

Walker, T., 52
White centering, 71
Work-study programs, 165

Yosso, T. J., 1, 12, 23, 24, 26, 28, 30, 33

About the Authors

Francisco Rios is emeritus professor and dean (retired) at Western Washington University. His research interests include Teachers of Color, Latinos in education, and preservice teacher education with a multicultural focus. Francisco served as president of the National Association for Multicultural Education from 2014–2016. He received the Distinguished Scholar Mid-Career Award from the Committee of Scholars of Color in Education from the American Educational Research Association. He is co-author with A Longoria of *Creating a Home in Schools: Sustaining Identities for Black, Indigenous, and Teachers of Color* (Teachers College Press, 2021). He remains active in community organization and development work locally and in Washington State.

Jacquelyn Bridgeman is the Kepler Professor of Law at the University of Wyoming. She earned her bachelor of arts degree with honors from Stanford University and her juris doctorate from the University of Chicago. Throughout her career she has held a number of administrative positions and taught courses in a range of disciplines inside and outside of the legal field. Before entering academia, she practiced law in Los Angeles, CA, and currently serves as the magistrate judge for the Integrated Juvenile Treatment Program for Albany County, WY. Her scholarly writing has been in the areas of race, gender, education, politics, family, and sports.

Angela M. Jaime (Enrolled member of the Pit River Tribe) is a professor and vice-provost, Indigenous engagement, at the University of Saskatchewan, Canada. She earned her bachelor of arts degree in Native American studies from California State University, Sacramento; master of arts degree in American Indian studies from San Francisco State University; and her PhD in education from Purdue University. Throughout her career as a scholar, educator, and administrator she has pursued paths for systems change to improve higher education for Indigenous and Students of Color. Her most important roles in life have been as a daughter to a loving and supportive mother and a mom to two amazing young men (Esai and Emiliano).

Kevin C. Roxas is a professor and dean of the Woodring College of Education at Western Washington University. His research focuses on collaborative engagement with immigrant students, their parents, and other family members as they use photography and visual and written narratives to powerfully describe their experiences in U.S. public schools and local communities. He is the editor of *Multicultural Perspectives*, the journal of the National Association of Multicultural Education. In 2019, the National Association of Multicultural Education (NAME) selected Roxas for the Carl A. Grant Outstanding Research Award. In 2023, the National Association of Multicultural Education (NAME) selected him for the Pritchy Smith Multicultural Educator of the Year Award.

Caskey Russell is the father of two sons and a professor of literature and Indigenous studies. He's an enrolled member of the Tlingit tribe (Eagle/Naasteidí) of Alaska. He received his BA and MA in English from Western Washington University, and his PhD from the University of Oregon. His dissertation examined Tlingit intellectual traditions. He taught at Iowa State University and the University of Wyoming and is currently dean of Fairhaven College at Western Washington University.